SO YOU THINK YOU'RE A DETROIT RED WINGS FAN?

STARS, STATS, RECORDS, AND MEMORIES FOR TRUE DIEHARDS

PAT GASS

SPORTS PUBLISHING

Sports Publishing books may be purchased in bulk at special discounts for sales promotion, corporate gifts, fund-raising, or educational purposes. Special editions can also be created to specifications. For details, contact the Special Sales Department, Sports Publishing, 307 West 36th Street, 11th Floor, New York, NY 10018 or sportspubbooks@skyhorsepublishing.com.

Sports Publishing® is a registered trademark of Skyhorse Publishing, Inc.®, a Delaware corporation.

Visit our website at www.sportspubbooks.com.

10 9 8 7 6 5 4 3 2 1

Library of Congress Cataloging-in-Publication Data is available on file.

Cover design by Tom Lau
Cover photo credit: Associated Press

ISBN: 978-1-68358-256-4
Ebook ISBN: 978-1-68358-257-1

Printed in the United States of America

Contents

Preface

A lot of my early memories of the Detroit Red Wings were painful ones. Watching the Wings in the late 1970s and much of the 1980s was frustrating, to say the least. The days of Gordie Howe, Terry Sawchuk, and the 1950s dynasty were long gone, and the Steve Yzerman-Nicklas Lidstrom teams of the 1990s and 2000s were still a long way away.

There never was, and never will be, another player like Howe. He had had plenty of help in the early 1950s, when Detroit won the Stanley Cup four times in six seasons while wearing those simple, classic, red-and-white uniforms with the winged wheel, a design that's changed little to the present day.

But when I began watching them, I didn't realize that the Red Wings were headed for their own low ebb. Despite the presence of stars such as Marcel Dionne and Mickey Redmond in the 1970s, and John Ogrodnick and a young Yzerman in the '80s, the Red Wings were lost in the NHL wilderness for most of those two decades.

It took a while after Mike Ilitch bought the team, but, by the 1990s, the Red Wings were relevant again. By the middle of the decade, they were in the Stanley Cup Final for the first time in 30 years, and, in 1997, the Cup returned to Detroit for the first time in 42 years.

Players like Yzerman, Lidstrom, Sergei Fedorov, Pavel Datsyuk, and Henrik Zetterberg triggered a stretch that saw the Red Wings win the Cup four times from 1997 to 2008 and get to Game Seven of the Final in 2009. With the passage of time, it's easier to see that those teams were among some of the best ever to take the ice.

The Red Wings performed one of hockey's great feats by qualifying for the playoffs for 25 consecutive seasons—something no NHL team has done since the 1990s wave of expansion began—before coming up short in 2016–17. The young talent in the system bodes well for a quick return to the top.

I owe a debt of thanks to Julie Ganz and the folks at Skyhorse Publishing for their hard work in sanding and polishing my raw product into the finished version you hold in your hands.

Now it's time to get ready. Strap on your shin guards, sharpen your skates, buckle up your helmet, and let's get started.

Introduction

Twenty-five consecutive years in the Stanley Cup Playoffs. Four championships in a span of 12 years. Those are some of the accomplishments fans of the Detroit Red Wings have seen in the past three decades.

The Red Wings have had two eras in which they were as good as any team that ever stepped onto an NHL rink. The Scotty Bowman/Mike Babcock–coached teams that helped turn Detroit into Hockeytown are familiar to most of today's fans, but the Red Wings of the early 1950s that won four Cups in six years were just as dominant (albeit in a league that was just six teams, rather than today's 31).

That team featured one of the NHL's greatest and best-named lines, the "Production Line" with Ted Lindsay, Gordie Howe, and Sid Abel. Alex Delvecchio later moved into the middle. Red Kelly was the Nicklas Lidstrom of his day, a smart, smooth-skating defenseman who was among the greats of his era. Terry Sawchuk was arguably the greatest goaltender of the Original Six era.

Of course, the NHL will never see another player like Howe, whose greatness on and off the ice earned him the nickname "Mr. Hockey." It was a perfect two-word description of a sports immortal.

The later era of Detroit dominance also had its stars. Steve Yzerman almost had two careers, one as one of the NHL's highest-scoring centers, the second as an elite two-way player and leader. Lidstrom was arguably the best defenseman of the past 40 years. Bowman and Babcock are among the greatest coaches in NHL history.

For nine decades, the Red Wings have been a pillar of the National Hockey League. In good times and not so good times, they've always been among hockey's most exciting teams.

And now on to this book. Just like a hockey game, the difficulty level of the questions you'll see will get tougher as you move along from the first period through the second and third, into overtime, and finally on to the shootout. We hope you'll have fun—and get a chance to prove to your friends what a great Red Wings fan you are!

FIRST PERIOD

The National Anthem has been sung, the officials are headed to their respective spots on the ice, and the full house at Little Caesars Arena is settling in for 60 minutes of action. We're ready for 40 questions in the first period, so drop the puck and let's go!

1 Few players are as identified with one franchise as Gordie Howe is with the Red Wings. Howe's No. 9 is among the numbers hanging from the rafters at Little Caesars Arena. But that wasn't his original number with the Red Wings. What was the first number he wore after joining Detroit in 1946? *Answer on page 11.*

a. No. 7
b. No. 12
c. No. 17
d. No. 21

2 Speaking of Mr. Hockey, he played 26 seasons in the NHL but scored more than 100 points exactly once. In which season did he reach triple figures? Give yourself a bonus point if you know how many he had! *Answer on page 11.*

3 The Red Wings set a single-season NHL record in 2016–17 for the most shootout victories without a loss. How many did they win? *Answer on page 12.*

a. 8
b. 9
c. 10
d. 11

1

4 Nicklas Lidstrom is one of the greatest defensemen in NHL history, and Red Wings fans got to see him spend his entire career in red and white. He was part of Detroit's famed 1989 draft class, one of the best in NHL history. In which round did the Red Wings select Lidstrom? *Answer on page 14.*

a. 1

b. 2

c. 3

d. 4

5 The Red Wings were in one of their down periods in the early 1980s, but they had the No. 4 pick in the 1983 NHL Draft, giving them the opportunity to acquire Steve Yzerman. Yet Yzerman wasn't really the player they wanted. Which player would have been taken by the Wings if things had worked out the way they had planned? (Hint: He was a pretty good player too!) *Answer on page 15.*

6 Pavel Datsyuk was a star for the Red Wings from his arrival in Detroit in 2001–02 to his departure after the 2015–16 season. He's also the most recent Red Wing to wear No. 13. How many other Detroit players have worn than number? *Answer on page 16.*

a. 0

b. 2

c. 4

d. 6

7 Mike Modano, a native of Livonia, Michigan, played a final season in Detroit after spending his NHL career with the Minnesota North Stars/Dallas Stars franchise. He had to change his number when he came to Detroit, because the No. 9 he'd worn throughout his career was no longer available. Which number did he opt for with the Red Wings? *Answer on page 17.*

a. 70
b. 80
c. 90
d. 91

8 Hall of Famer Scotty Bowman capped his coaching career by leading the Red Wings to the Stanley Cup in 2002. Who succeeded him? *Answer on page 18.*
a. Mike Babcock
b. Jacques Demers
c. Dave Lewis
d. Brian Murray

9 Gordie Howe wasn't the only Red Wings great with that last name. Syd Howe (no relation) helped Detroit win the Stanley Cup three times and retired after the 1945–46 season as the leading scorer in NHL history. And though Gordie Howe holds a host of team records, Syd Howe did something that Gordie couldn't. What was it? *Answer on page 20.*

10 The Red Wings are the only team in NHL history to win the Stanley Cup by scoring in overtime of Game Seven in the Final. How many times have they done so? *Answer on page 21.*
a. 1
b. 2
c. 3
d. 4

11 The Red Wings set team records for most penalty minutes and most losses in the same season. When was it? *Answer on page 24.*
a. 1975–76
b. 1981–82
c. 1985–86
d. 1986–87

12 2016–17 was the Red Wings' final season at Joe Louis Arena. The last game was played on April 9, 2017. Who was the opponent in that game? *Answer on page 25.*
   a. New Jersey Devils
   b. New York Rangers
   c. Philadelphia Flyers
   d. Toronto Maple Leafs

13 No. 1 was retired in honor of Terry Sawchuk on March 6, 1994, 30 years after he last wore it with the Red Wings. A total of 10 other goaltenders wore No. 1 after Sawchuk. Who was the last one? *Answer on page 26.*
   a. Hank Bassen
   b. Gilles Gilbert
   c. Glen Hanlon
   d. Corrado Micalef

14 Kris Draper was one of the NHL's best defensive centers during his 17 seasons with the Red Wings, winning the Selke Trophy in 2004. He spent the first three seasons of his NHL career with the Winnipeg Jets. What did the Red Wings give up to get him? *Answer on page 27.*

15 Which of the following players was *not* a member of the "Russian Five?" *Answer on page 29.*
   a. Pavel Datsyuk
   b. Vladimir Konstantinov
   c. Vyacheslav Kozlov
   d. Igor Larionov

16 The Red Wings won the Stanley Cup in 1997 and 1998. How many games did they lose in the two Finals against the Philadelphia Flyers in '97 and the Washington Capitals in '98? *Answer on page 31.*

a. 0
b. 1
c. 2
d. 3

17 The Red Wings made a blockbuster trade in 1996 that brought Brendan Shanahan to Detroit. But which future Hall of Famer went the other way, from the Red Wings to the Whalers? *Answer on page 33.*
a. Chris Chelios
b. Paul Coffey
c. Sergei Fedorov
d. Larry Murphy

18 Among Gordie Howe's numerous accomplishments was the NHL's longest streak of consecutive top-five finishes in the scoring race. How many consecutive seasons did Howe finish among the NHL's top-five scorers? *Answer on page 35.*
a. 16
b. 18
c. 20
d. 22

19 Two of the seven players in NHL history to score 700 or more goals got goal No. 700 while playing for the Red Wings. One was Gordie Howe. Who was the other? *Answer on page 36.*
a. Marcel Dionne
b. Brett Hull
c. Brendan Shanahan
d. Steve Yzerman

20 The Red Wings had a Hall of Fame defense pairing during their championship seasons of 1996–97 and 1997–98. Nicklas Lidstrom was a career Red Wing. Who was his regular partner during those seasons? *Answer on page 37.*

a. Viacheslav Fetisov
b. Vladimir Konstantinov
c. Niklas Kronwall
d. Larry Murphy

21 What was the name of the line formed by Ted Lindsay, Sid Abel, and Gordie Howe? *Answer on page 38.*
a. The Bread Line
b. The Production Line
c. The Punch Line
d. The Winged Wheelers

22 Speaking of Lindsay, what was his nickname? *Answer on page 39.*
a. Terrible Ted
b. Tough Teddy
c. Super 7
d. The Captain

23 Who is the only Red Wings goaltender to score a goal? *Answer on page 41.*
a. Dominik Hasek
b. Jimmy Howard
c. Petr Mrazek
d. Chris Osgood

24 In what year did Mike and Marian Ilitch purchase the Red Wings? *Answer on page 42.*
a. 1980
b. 1982
c. 1984
d. 1986

25 Who is the longest-serving employee in the history of the Red Wings? *Answer on page 44.*
   a. Jack Adams
   b. Jim Devellano
   c. Gordie Howe
   d. Steve Yzerman

26 Which team spent the most consecutive seasons as a Red Wings farm team? *Answer on page 46.*
   a. Adirondack Red Wings
   b. Grand Rapids Griffins
   c. Indianapolis Capitals
   d. Toledo Walleye

27 At which college did Jeff Blashill coach before he joined the Red Wings? *Answer on page 47.*
   a. Michigan State
   b. Michigan Tech
   c. Northern Michigan
   d. Western Michigan

28 Forward Anthony Mantha isn't the first player in his family to play for the Red Wings. Mantha's paternal grandfather, a former Red Wing, was actually in attendance to see Anthony's first NHL goal. Who is he? *Answer on page 48.*

29 Gustav Nyquist is a native of Sweden but played college hockey in the United States. Where did he play? *Answer on page 49.*
   a. Boston College
   b. Boston University
   c. Holy Cross
   d. University of Maine

30 The Red Wings locked up Henrik Zetterberg for a long time when they signed him to a contract on January 28, 2009. How long is the contract? *Answer on page 49.*
a. 8 years
b. 10 years
c. 12 years
d. 14 years

31 A big part of the Red Wings' success under Scotty Bowman came after he brought in a new system. What was it called? *Answer on page 51.*
a. Firewagon hockey
b. Four corners
c. Left-wing lock
d. Neutral-zone trap

32 The Red Wings had a brilliant decade under coach Mike Babcock, winning the Stanley Cup in 2008, nearly repeating in 2009 and qualifying for the Stanley Cup Playoffs in all 10 of his seasons behind the bench. The Wings were Babcock's second NHL coaching job. Which team did he coach before coming to Detroit? *Answer on page 53.*
a. Chicago Blackhawks
b. Florida Panthers
c. Mighty Ducks of Anaheim
d. Toronto Maple Leafs

33 The Red Wings have enjoyed success in their home opener since entering the NHL in 1926. With a 3-2 overtime loss to the Columbus Blue Jackets to begin the 2018–19 season, how many consecutive years have the Red Wings gone without a regulation loss in their home opener? *Answer on page 54.*

a. 5
b. 6
c. 7
d. 8

34 The Red Wings have a winning record on all of these special occasions except one. Which one is it? *Answer on page 56.*
   a. Halloween
   b. New Year's Eve
   c. St. Patrick's Day
   d. Easter

35 Three Red Wings coaches have won more than 400 regular-season games. Which one of these did not? *Answer on page 57.*
   a. Sid Abel
   b. Jack Adams
   c. Mike Babcock
   d. Scotty Bowman

36 Before Steve Yzerman spent an incredible 19 seasons as captain of the Red Wings, which Detroit player had worn the "C" for the longest time? *Answer on page 58.*
   a. Sid Abel
   b. Alex Delvecchio
   c. Gordie Howe
   d. Ted Lindsay

37 The Red Wings set an NHL record during the 2011–12 season for the longest home winning streak in league history. How long was the streak? Extra points if you know when it started and ended. *Answer on page 60.*
   a. 19 games
   b. 21 games
   c. 23 games
   d. 25 games

38 The Red Wings' franchise record for the fastest two goals scored is five seconds, which they've done twice. Which player was involved in each instance? *Answer on page 62.*
a. Todd Bertuzzi
b. Pavel Datsyuk
c. Tomas Holmstrom
d. Nicklas Lidstrom

39 Gordie Howe and Steve Yzerman share one team career record. What is it? *Answer on page 63.*
a. Assists
b. Games played
c. Hat tricks
d. Power-play goals

40 Only one member of the Red Wings has scored goals in nine consecutive games—and he's done it twice. Who is he? *Answer on page 64.*
a. Gordie Howe
b. Ted Lindsay
c. Mickey Redmond
d. Steve Yzerman

There's the horn. The first period is over. Take a break and come back ready for the second period.

FIRST PERIOD—
ANSWERS

1 Few players are as identified with a particular number as Gordie Howe is with No. 9. But it's not the only number he wore while playing for the Red Wings.

Howe was wearing No. 17 when he made his NHL debut and scored a goal against the Toronto Maple Leafs on October 16, 1946, and he wore it throughout the 1946–47 season, when he scored seven goals and finished with 22 points in 58 games.

Howe didn't don No. 9 until his second season with Detroit. He reportedly was perfectly happy with the number he had and didn't want the change until he was told that the lower number would give him a lower berth in the Pullman car the Red Wings used on road trips during the era in which teams did most of their travel by train.

Of course, Howe went on to wear No. 9 until he finally hung up his skates in 1980.

"It's a pretty classic number, and a lot of great players have worn it, but what it meant to me was that I got a better night's sleep," Howe told the *National Post* in 2014. "Many people may not know that my first number with the Red Wings was No. 17 until early into my first season. The No. 9 became available, and it was offered to me. We traveled by train back then, and guys with higher numbers got the top bunk on the sleeper car. No. 9 meant I got a lower berth on the train, which was much nicer than crawling into the top bunk."

2 It seems incredible that Gordie Howe's NHL career included just one 100-point season. Then again, he wasn't playing today's 82-game seasons. When Howe came to the NHL in 1946, the season was 60 games long, and from 1949–50 through 1966–67, teams played 70 games. Howe led the NHL in scoring six times during that span, finishing with anywhere from 81 to 95 points. Projected over an 82-game season, that range would be 95 to 112 points.

But in terms of actually producing 100 points, it didn't happen until 1968–69, when Howe finished with 103 (44 goals, 59 assists). Perhaps most amazing is that he did it by getting four points (two goals, two assists) in the Red Wings' final game of the season against the Chicago Black Hawks (as they were known then) on March 30, 1969, just one day after his 41st birthday.

Howe's 100th point came when he scored 33 seconds into the second period, beating Chicago goaltender Denis DeJordy.

But he wasn't done there. Howe scored his 44th goal of the season by beating DeJordy at 11:02 during a Detroit power play.

His 102nd and 103rd points came when he assisted on third-period goals by Frank Mahovlich and Garry Unger, capping a late-season surge in which Howe piled up 15 points (six goals, nine assists) in Detroit's final nine games.

The only downside to Howe's record is that his historic night came in a 9–5 loss at Chicago Stadium, one that capped a season in which Detroit finished 33–31–12 and failed to qualify for the Stanley Cup Playoffs.

That 103-point season was the biggest of Mr. Hockey's pro career and his only 100-point performance in the NHL. However, he did reach the 100-point mark twice while playing for the Houston Aeros of the World Hockey Association. In 1973–74, his first season in the WHA after returning to the ice following a two-year retirement, Howe finished with an even 100 points (31 goals, 69 assists) in 70 games. Two years later, Howe put up 102 points (32 goals, 70 assists) in 78 games, superb numbers for a player of any age, but almost incomprehensible for someone who had turned 47 just before the end of the regular season.

3 The NHL instituted the shootout in 2005 in order to eliminate ties. The league eliminated overtime in 1942 to accommodate travel schedules during World War II; in 1983, it brought back a five-minute, sudden-death OT in which the winner got two points in the standings and the loser none (each team got a point in the standings if no one scored and the game ended in a tie). In 1999–2000, the NHL changed the rules to give the losing team one point in the standings, while also reducing the number of skaters for each team from five to four.

The Red Wings weren't particularly successful in shootouts from 2005 to 2016. They were 49–65, and at one point in calendar year 2013, lost 11 consecutive shootouts.

Detroit won its first shootout of the 2015–16 season, lost the next five, and won the last one, 2–1, against the Columbus Blue Jackets on February 23, 2016. Maybe that was an omen of better things to come, because in 2016–17, the Red Wings were *unbeatable* in the tiebreaker.

Their first shootout was an eight-round marathon against the St. Louis Blues at Scottrade Center on October 27, 2016. Petr Mrazek gave up a goal to Alexander Steen in the first round but was perfect through the next seven. Gustav Nyquist scored in the second round for Detroit, and Henrik Zetterberg got the winner in the bottom of the eighth round for a 2–1 win.

The next two shootouts were also on the road, with Jimmy Howard in goal. Andreas Athanasiou scored the only goal in Philadelphia on November 8, and Thomas Vanek got the winner on November 23 at Buffalo.

The Red Wings improved to 5–0 with two more road wins in December. Vanek scored in the third round and Zetterberg in the fourth for a 4–3 win at Winnipeg, with Mrazek in goal, on December 6. Vanek scored again against the Florida Panthers 17 days later before Frans Nielsen got the deciding goal in another 4–3 win, this one with rookie Jared Coreau in goal.

The home fans finally got a look at the Red Wings' shootout mastery on January 18. With Mrazek in goal, Vanek and Nielsen scored to give Detroit a 6–5 win against the Boston Bruins. Exactly one month later, Zetterberg scored his third game-deciding goal, this one in the fifth round, to give the Red Wings a 3–2 win against the Washington Capitals.

Nyquist scored the only goal and Mrazek didn't allow one in three tries to give Detroit a 5–4 win against the Coyotes in Glendale, Arizona, on March 16. The Red Wings completed their 9–0 season in the shootout on April 3, when rookie Evgeny Svechnikov scored the only goal in a seven-round tiebreaker that gave Detroit a 5–4 victory against the Ottawa Senators in what proved to be the final shootout at Joe Louis Arena.

The final shootout tally for the 2016–17 season: The Red Wings were 6–0 on the road, 3–0 at home. Mrazek was 6–0, Howard 2–0 and Coreau 1–0. Zetterberg led the way with three game-deciding goals, and Nielsen had two. Mrazek's .867 save percentage—four goals on 30 shots—was the best in the NHL among goaltenders who took part in more than three shootouts.

Those two goals by Nielsen were the only successes he had in eight attempts—the worst shootout season in his career. He signed with the Red Wings on July 2, 2016, after a decade with the New York Islanders during which he was 42-for-82 with 19 deciding goals, the most successful shooter in the history of the tiebreaker.

4 Nicklas Lidstrom has arguably been the NHL's best defenseman during the past four decades (since the retirement of Bobby Orr). He won the Norris Trophy as the NHL's top blueliner seven times, more than anyone other than Orr, and was a cornerstone of the Red Wings' championship teams in 1997, 1998, 2002, and 2008. He was inducted into the Hockey Hall of Fame in 2015, the first year he was eligible, and was named to the 100 Greatest NHL Players in 2017.

With credentials like that, you'd think Lidstrom would have been a first-round choice when he became eligible for the NHL draft, in 1989. But he wasn't. In fact, he wasn't taken in the second round either.

It was all due to a little bit of intrigue.

It seems the Red Wings had unearthed Lidstrom in Sweden but were desperate to keep their interest a secret in order to be able to pick him lower in the draft (try getting away with that today). The Wings had him targeted for the third round, the last one, at the time, in which 18 year olds could be drafted.

"The draft wasn't as big as it is now," Lidstrom told NHL.com. "My agent [Don Meehan] wanted to bring me over here and be part of the draft, but the Red Wings said they didn't want anyone else to see that I was here, because someone else might pick me ahead of them. I was at home with my agent, and the Red Wings told me to wait by the phone, and they finally did pick me. Christer Rockstrom, who scouts for the Red Wings, scouted me."

Neil Smith, who went on to build the New York Rangers' Stanley Cup-winning team in 1994, was part of a trio of Detroit executives, along with Rockstrom and general manager Jim Devellano, who knew about Lidstrom. None of them was saying anything.

"He certainly wasn't a physical killer," Smith said years later. "He had a great understanding of the game. Nobody could beat him. Just think of a younger version of what you saw in the league all those years."

The hard part was keeping the rest of the league from stealing Lidstrom away.

"I knew that if we didn't take him in the third round this year, he'd go in the first round next year, because he'll play in the World Junior [Championship] for Sweden and then everybody will know about him," said Smith, who also pleaded with Meehan not to bring Lidstrom to the draft. Meehan complied, and the Red Wings got one of the all-time steals.

After taking center Mike Sillinger in the first round and defenseman Bob Boughner in the second, the Red Wings selected Lidstrom with the 11th selection (53rd overall) in the third round. Years later, Smith called it the best pick of his career. Given the results, it's hard to argue with him.

5 The rejuvenation of the Red Wings began in the 1983 NHL Draft. Detroit had the fourth choice in the first round, and new general manager Jim Devellano, who had been hired after he'd helped Bill Torrey build the New York Islanders' dynasty teams of the early 1980s, had his eye on a dynamic 18-year-old center named Pat LaFontaine.

Not only was LaFontaine a premier scorer, he'd grown up in Waterford, Michigan, and had played in the Detroit area before spending the 1982–83 season torching the Quebec Major Junior Hockey League while playing for Verdun. If ever there was a perfect match of player and team, this seemed to be it. Not only would the Red Wings get a future star, they'd get one who could help sell tickets at Joe Louis Arena, which was often half-empty back then.

The problem was getting the chance to take him. The Minnesota North Stars (now the Dallas Stars) had their eyes on US high-school star Brian Lawton with the No. 1 pick, but the Hartford Whalers, picking second, were regarded by many as likely to take LaFontaine with the No. 2 choice.

"I had approached the three teams ahead of me, asking what it would take to flip-flop picks," Devellano said. But none of the teams ahead of the Red Wings was interested in dealing.

To the surprise of many, the Whalers took forward Sylvain Turgeon with the second choice. That left Devellano's old team, the Islanders, next on the clock. The Islanders, coming off their fourth straight Stanley Cup championship, had fleeced the Colorado Rockies (who later moved to New Jersey) in a 1981 trade, dealing two spare parts—defenseman Bob Lorimer and forward Dave Cameron—for Colorado's first-round pick in 1983. That turned out to be the third choice—and Torrey, Devellano's old boss, decided that LaFontaine was just the player he needed to help keep the dynasty going.

However, Devellano didn't go on to a Hall of Fame career by being unprepared. Though "Jimmy D" later admitted he'd have taken LaFontaine had he been available, he had a Plan B ready to go. That plan turned out to be Yzerman, a skinny, 175-pound center who had put up 91 points (42 goals, 49 assists) in 56 games for Peterborough of the Ontario Hockey League in 1982–83.

"We feel he can contribute right away," Devellano said after the draft. "My only concern is that because of his age—he's only 18—his strength is a question mark. But I think he's gonna make it."

6 Pavel Datsyuk arrived in Detroit just in time to grab No. 13.

Datsyuk was the 171st player taken in the 1998 NHL Draft, a kid from Sverdlovsk, Russia, who was allowed to mature in his home country by the talent-laden Red Wings until they brought him to North America in 2001.

That was just in time to nab No. 13, which had been left open by a trade that sent forward Vyacheslav Kozlov to the Buffalo Sabres as part of the package that brought goaltender Dominik Hasek to the Wings. Kozlov had been a two-time 30-goal scorer for the Red Wings and a valuable member of their Stanley Cup-winning teams in 1997 and 1998. But he'd scored just 18 goals in 1999–2000 and 20 in 2000–01, and the Wings deemed him expendable (partly because they knew that Datsyuk was in the pipeline).

Kozlov had worn No. 13 from the time he joined the Red Wings for seven games in the 1991–92 season, making him the third Detroit player to wear what many players deemed "unlucky No. 13."

The first Red Wing to wear No. 13 didn't do so for long.

Harold "Gizzy" Hart was a left wing who played for Detroit (then known as the Cougars) during 1926–27, the franchise's inaugural season. He had spent the previous three seasons with the Victoria Cougars of the Western Hockey League and came to Detroit after the WHL went out of business.

Hart's time with the Red Wings was short. After he went without a point in two games, Detroit sold Hart to the Montreal Canadiens on December 12, 1926. Hart played the rest of the 1926–27 season and all of 1927–28 with the Canadiens, returned to the minors with the Providence Reds from 1928 to 1932, and then returned to the Canadiens for 18 games in 1932–33. He went back to the minor league Reds until 1934, then spent his final career season of 1937–38 with the Southern Saskatchewan Senior Hockey League's (SSSHL's) Weyburn Beavers.

Hart was the only Red Wing to wear No. 13 until Kozlov did so in 1991.

7 Mike Modano was already the highest-scoring NHL player born in the United States when he came home to the Red Wings in 2010. Modano had played for Detroit Compuware in 1985–86, finishing with 66 goals and 131 points before going to spend three seasons with Prince Albert of the Western Hockey League. His 47-goal,

127-point season in 1987–88 attracted the attention of the Minnesota North Stars, who took him with the No. 1 pick in the 1988 NHL Draft.

Modano signed with the North Stars on Christmas Day in 1988, joined them for two playoff games in 1989, then became a full-time NHL player in 1989–90, finishing his rookie season with 29 goals and 75 points.

He became the face of the franchise after the North Stars became the Dallas Stars in 1993 and helped carry them to the Stanley Cup in 1999 (still the only Cup in that team's history). He played all six games in the Final against the Buffalo Sabres despite a broken wrist sustained in Game 2. He had seven points (all assists) in the Final and led the Stars in the playoffs with 23 points.

But the Stars announced after the 2009–10 season that they wouldn't re-sign Modano, and after deciding he wanted to continue playing, Modano signed a one-year contract with the Red Wings. The No. 9 he's worn in Minnesota and Dallas had long since been retired in Detroit in honor of Gordie Howe, so Modano opted to wear No. 90.

Coach Mike Babcock planned to have Modano center the third line between Dan Cleary and Jiri Hudler. He got off to a sensational start, taking a pass from Cleary and scoring against the Anaheim Ducks at 5:35 of the first period in Detroit's season opener on October 8, 2010, at Joe Louis Arena, sparking his new team to a 4–0 win. But Modano wound up being limited to 40 games during the 2010–11 season after a skate severed a tendon in his right wrist. He finished the season with four goals and 15 points, giving him 561 goals and 1,374 points in 1,499 regular-season games during 21 seasons. He was inducted into the Hockey Hall of Fame in November 2014, and he was named to the 100 Greatest NHL Players in 2017.

8 Dave Lewis never spent a day in the minor leagues. He played 1,008 NHL games doing one of hockey's most thankless jobs, being a defensive defenseman. Lewis never scored more than five goals or had more than 29 points in his 15 NHL seasons, the last two of which were spent with the Red Wings.

His playing career ended after he dressed for six games with Detroit during the 1987–88 season, but his involvement with the team didn't. The Red Wings hired him as an assistant under coach Jacques Demers.

Lewis remained as an assistant after Bryan Murray took over as coach in 1990 and was kept when Scotty Bowman succeeded Murray in 1993. Lewis was promoted to associate coach in 1995, largely focusing on the defense, and was part of the Red Wings during their Stanley Cup-winning seasons in 1996–97, 1997–98, and 2001–02.

When Bowman called it a career after the Wings won the Cup in 2002, Lewis was the logical successor. He got the job on July 17, 2002.

The Red Wings had an excellent first season under Lewis, finishing first in the Central Division, second in the Western Conference, and third in the overall NHL standings at 48–20–10–4 (110 points). They appeared to have an excellent chance to repeat as Stanley Cup champions, only to run into the seventh-seeded Anaheim Ducks, who got a brilliant effort by goaltender Jean-Sebastian Giguere and swept the Western Conference Quarterfinal series in four games, one of the most stunning upsets in playoff history.

But Detroit showed no ill effects from the stunning playoff loss in 2003–04. The Red Wings went 48–21–11–2 that season, winning the Central Division again and finishing first in the NHL standings. This time, they got past the first round of the playoffs, defeating the pesky Nashville Predators in six games. But they came up short in the Western Conference Semifinals, losing to the Calgary Flames in six games. The series was tied 2–2 after four games, but Flames goaltender Miikka Kiprusoff made 31 saves in a 1–0 victory in Game 5 at Joe Louis Arena, and Calgary won, 1–0, in overtime in Game 6.

The lockout that shut down the NHL for the 2004–05 season spelled the end to Lewis's coaching career in Detroit. His contract was allowed to run out on June 30, 2005, and he was rehired as a scout on August 9, 2005.

Lewis spent one season as a Wings scout before being hired as coach of the Boston Bruins in 2006, but he was let go after the Bruins went 35–41–6 in 2006–07 and missed the playoffs. Since then, he's been an assistant with the Los Angeles Kings and Carolina Hurricanes, and he has coached the national teams of Ukraine and Belarus.

9 For all of Gordie Howe's brilliance during his 25 seasons with the Red Wings, he never scored more than three goals in a single game. Mr. Hockey had 19 regular-season hat tricks and one in the Stanley Cup Playoffs on April 10, 1954.

He'd have had to combine two of those hat tricks to equal the performance that Syd Howe (no relation) had against the New York Rangers on February 3, 1944.

Less than two weeks after Syd scored three times against the lowly Rangers—they finished that season 6–39–5—in Detroit's historic 15–0 win on January 23, 1944, he doubled that feat during the Red Wings' 12–2 win at the Olympia.

In front of a crowd of 12,293, the Red Wings were already leading, 1–0, when Howe scored his 18th goal of the season, beating goaltender Ken McAuley at 11:27. His second goal of the night came 18 seconds later and gave the Red Wings a 3–0 lead after one period.

The game was still 3–0 late in the second period when Howe completed his seventh regular-season hat trick by scoring at 17:52. Goal number four came 62 seconds later, and Cully Simon scored with four seconds remaining in the period for a 6–0 lead.

After Mud Bruneteau made it 7–0 early in the third period, Howe struck for two more quick goals to complete his historic night. Don Grasso and Bruneteau each assisted, when Howe scored first at 8:17 and again at 9:14

"They were going in the net tonight," said Howe, who was carried off the ice on the shoulders of his teammates. "I don't remember any goal in particular. The boys were feeding them to me nicely.

"No celebration for me," he added, according to the *Detroit News*, "I'm due at work at 7:10 a.m."

Howe worked as a machinist at Ford Motor Company by day, playing center and left wing by night.

He became the first NHL player to score six goals in a game since Cy Denneny of the Ottawa Senators had done it on March 7, 1921. Only two players since Howe have scored six goals in a game: Red Berenson of the St. Louis Blues did it against the Philadelphia Flyers on November 7, 1968, and Darryl Sittler of the Toronto Maple Leafs scored six goals during his NHL record 10-point night against the Boston Bruins on February 7, 1976.

Oddly enough, Howe didn't have the biggest offensive performance on the Red Wings that night. Grasso had one goal of his own and assisted on six others, including five by Howe, for seven points. Perhaps incredibly, Howe also scored all six of his goals without benefit of a power play; the Rangers didn't take a penalty all night.

10 Game 7 of the Stanley Cup Final is one of the ultimate contests in any sport. Having the most important game of the season go into overtime ups the pressure exponentially.

Such a scenario had never happened from the time the NHL went to a best-of-seven format in the Final in 1939 until 1950, when the Red Wings played the New York Rangers.

On paper, it was a series that should never have gone to a seventh game. The Red Wings had run away with first place, finishing the 70-game season with 88 points—remember, there was no overtime or shootouts used to determine a winner if the game was tied after 60 minutes during that era—while the Rangers were a distant fourth with 67. But the Rangers upset the Montreal Canadiens in the Semifinals, winning in five games behind the goaltending of Chuck Rayner, who won the Hart Trophy as regular-season MVP. The Red Wings had to go seven games to eliminate the Toronto Maple Leafs and needed to win Games 6 (4–0 at Toronto) and 7 (1–0 at Detroit on an overtime goal by Leo Reise).

They'd lost Gordie Howe in Game 1, when Howe missed his check on Leafs center Ted "Teeder" Kennedy and went face-first into the boards. Howe was carried off the ice with a badly broken skull and didn't play again until the following season. But in Detroit's favor, the Rangers wouldn't get to play a home game. With the circus taking over Madison Square Garden, the Rangers were the "home" team for Games 2 and 3 at Maple Leaf Gardens in Toronto, with all other games at the Olympia.

The series started according to form, with Detroit winning the opener, 4–1. The Rangers won, 3–1, in Game 2, but a 4–0 win in Game 3 sent the series back to Detroit with the Red Wings poised to close it out quickly. But that didn't happen, largely thanks to Rayner and New York center Don Raleigh, who scored in overtime for a 3–2 win in Game 4, then did it again in OT for a 2–1 win in Game 5, becoming the first player to score back-to-back overtime goals in the Final in the process.

The Red Wings were on the ropes when the Rangers took 2–0 and 3–1 leads in Game 6, then fell behind again when Tony Leswick scored 1:54 into the third period to give New York a 4–3 lead. But Ted Lindsay scored less than three minutes later to get the Wings even, and Sid Abel's goal midway through the third period stood up for a 5–4 win.

One night later, on April 23, 1950, the Red Wings again found themselves playing from behind, when New York scored two power-play goals in a 64-second span for a 2–0 lead after one period. Pete Babando and Abel scored power-play goals 21 seconds apart early in the second period to tie the game, and after Buddy O'Connor's goal midway through the period put New York back in front, Jim Peters scored at 15:57 to get the Red Wings even at 3–3.

The goalies took over after that, with Rayner and Detroit's Harry Lumley matching saves through a scoreless third period and a first 20-minute overtime.

Raleigh nearly got his third OT winner, but his shot hit the post. Not long afterward, George Gee won a faceoff back to Babando, whose backhander beat Rayner at 8:31 of the second overtime to give the Red Wings the Cup—and the longest Game 7 OT win in Final history.

"We were at a faceoff in their end to Rayner's right," Babando remembered in a 2000 interview with Mike Gibb of *The Hockey News*.

"I was playing with Gerry Couture and George Gee, who took the faceoff. Usually, George had me stand behind him. But this time he moved me over to the right and told me he was going to pull it that way. I had to take one stride and get it on my backhand. I let the shot go, and it went in."

Ironically, Leswick, who nearly cost the Red Wings the Cup in 1950, was their overtime hero four years later.

The Wings again were coming off a first-place season when they entered the 1954 Stanley Cup Playoffs. They had no problem polishing off the Maple Leafs in five games in the Semifinals and appeared ready to do the same in the Final against the Canadiens after winning Games 3 and 4 at the Forum. But with the packed house at the Olympia ready to celebrate, the Canadiens spoiled the party with a 1–0 win on an overtime goal by Ken Mosdell. Given new life, the Canadiens returned home and evened the series with a 4–1 win, with Floyd Curry scoring twice.

The full house at the Olympia for Game 7 on April 16, 1954, groaned when Curry scored midway through the first period to give the Canadiens a 1–0 lead. But Red Kelly tied the game, 1–1, at 1:17 of the second period by scoring a power-play goal.

After that, the goaltenders took over. Montreal's Gerry McNeil and Detroit's Terry Sawchuk were perfect through the rest of the second period and all of the third, sending Game 7 to overtime for the second time in four years.

Unlike the OT in the 1950 Final, this Game 7 ended quickly. Just over four minutes into overtime, Glen Skov carried the puck into the Montreal zone. The puck came to Leswick, who floated a long shot from near the right point toward the net.

It was a shot that McNeil normally would have handled easily. But Canadiens defenseman Doug Harvey tried to knock the puck down with his glove so he could play it; instead, he deflected the shot over McNeil's shoulder and into the net at 4:29.

Incredibly, the hero of the night never saw the Cup-winning goal.

"I had the puck around center ice or so, and I just wanted to do the smart thing and throw it in. If I get caught with the puck and the

Canadiens steal it, we may get caught and they may get an odd-man break," Leswick remembered years later. "Just like that, the game could be over. So I'm just thinking of lifting the puck down deep in their end, just making the safe play. I flipped it in nice and high and turned to get off the ice. The next thing I know, everyone's celebrating. It had gone in. I said, 'You've *got* to be kidding. It went in? Get out of here!'"

The crowd was stunned, then erupted as they realized what had happened. Irvin and the Canadiens stormed off the ice, refusing the traditional end-of-series handshake line.

No Game 7 of the Final has gone to overtime since then.

11 The Red Wings had no trouble filling the penalty box during the 1985–86 season. Winning games was another matter.

Detroit took a mind-boggling 2,393 penalty minutes in 1985–86; that's just under 30 minutes per game in an 80-game season. For perspective, the 2017–18 Red Wings played two more games but took a total of 710 penalty minutes, fewer than nine per game.

Joe Kocur led the 1985–86 Wings with 377 penalty minutes. No one else reached 200; however, nine other players took more than 100 minutes in penalties. Two of them (Warren Young and Gerard Gallant) each scored more than 20 goals despite taking more than 100 PIM.

But while the Philadelphia Flyers of the mid-1970s combined high penalty numbers with success in the standings, the 1985–86 Red Wings decidedly did not.

The Wings finished with a woeful record of 17–57–6; their 40 points were 14 fewer than the next-worst team (the Los Angeles Kings). The 57 losses are the most in franchise history.

Detroit had a losing record in every month except November, when the Red Wings went 5–5–2. They were 4–12 in games decided by one goal, and a mind-boggling 8–33 in games decided by three or more goals (meaning that more than half of Detroit's games were blowouts by the NHL's standard).

The parade to the penalty box was a big reason for Detroit's inability to win. Detroit was short-handed 394 times and allowed a league-leading 111 power-play goals, another team record. Their 71.8 penalty-killing percentage was next to last in the NHL.

Put that together with a leaky defense at even strength, and the Red Wings ended up setting a dubious team record by allowing an NHL-worst 415 goals, 98 more than the NHL average that season. Combine with a league-low 266 goals scored, and it's easy to see why Detroit came in 21st in a 21-team league.

12 All good things must come to an end, and that included the Red Wings' time at Joe Louis Arena. With the Wings missing the Stanley Cup Playoffs for the first time since 1990, it became obvious in the final weeks of the 2016–17 NHL season that their final game at "The Joe" would be April 9, 2017, when the New Jersey Devils came to town.

Rather than a wake, the Red Wings' 4–1 victory was treated more like a party with 20,027 guests and one of the staples of Detroit hockey: The team website reported that 35 octopuses hit the ice during the final game.

The outcome was almost immaterial. Neither the Red Wings nor Devils had been close to the playoff race for weeks, but Detroit's 4–1 win gave the fans one last chance to cheer.

"It was a perfect ending to an otherwise not-so-good season," captain Henrik Zetterberg said. "When you picture the last game at the Joe—except if it would've been Game 7 of the Stanley Cup Final—this was very nice."

Fans gave the Wings a standing ovation when they took the ice for warmups. Longtime star Steve Yzerman was cheered when he dropped the ceremonial first puck between Zetterberg and Devils captain Andy Greene.

"I thought it was a great building to play in," Yzerman said. "Every time you stepped on the ice for a game, you were always excited to play the game. It just had a really nice atmosphere in there. It was beautiful in its simplicity."

It was a doubly special night for Zetterberg, who was playing his 1,000th NHL game—all with the Red Wings.

"I've never had goose bumps that many times during a hockey game in my entire life," said Zetterberg, who received a Rolex watch from the team in a pregame ceremony. "It was an incredible night."

It was certainly a night that Detroit center Riley Sheahan would never forget. Sheahan came into the game having gone without a goal for the entire 2016–17 season, but he scored for the first time in exactly a year at 7:09 of the first period when he fired a wrist shot into the top of the net. Sheahan also had the honor of scoring the last goal in the arena's history when he connected during a power play with 2:33 remaining in the third period.

"There are a lot of things I will remember about my career, and scoring the last goal here will definitely be one of them," he said. "I'll have that for the rest of my life."

13 Terry Sawchuk and No. 1 were synonymous in Detroit during his first two stints with the Red Wings, 1949–50 through 1954–55 and 1957–58 through 1963–64. He had a goals-against average of less than 2.00 in each of his first five seasons with the Red Wings and wore the Winged Wheel for most of his Hall of Fame career.

But all good things come to an end, and the concept of retiring or honoring numbers wasn't prevalent when Sawchuk was claimed by the Toronto Maple Leafs in the NHL intraleague draft on June 10, 1964. In fact, seven other players had worn that number—Glenn Hall for the two seasons that Sawchuk spent with the Boston Bruins (1955–56 and 1956–57) and six others for brief stints while they filled in for Sawchuk.

This was an era in which teams usually had an unquestioned starter in goal—and that player usually wore No. 1. Thus, after Sawchuk left for Toronto, the Red Wings wasted no time reissuing it. The recipient was Sawchuk's replacement, Roger Crozier, who wore No. 1 from 1964–65 through 1969–70. Crozier even kept No. 1 when the Red Wings brought back Sawchuk for the 1968–69 season, with Sawchuk wearing No. 29.

Five players wore No. 1 during the next 10 seasons, with Jim Rutherford mostly owning it from 1974–75 through 1979–80 after wearing it briefly in 1970–71. Rutherford was still wearing No. 1 when he was traded to the Los Angeles Kings on March 10, 1981.

Gilles Gilbert, who had been wearing No. 30, switched to No. 1 when it became available, and he wore it until he retired after the 1982–83 season. Rutherford, who signed with Detroit for a last hurrah in the summer of 1982, wore No. 29 in his final appearance with the Wings.

Gilbert's retirement left No. 1 available for Corrado Micalef, who wore it for the next three seasons. But Micalef was demoted to the minors after going 1–9–1 during the 1985–86 season. The Red Wings acquired Glen Hanlon in a trade with the New York Rangers on July 29, 1986, and Hanlon wore No. 1 during his five seasons in Detroit before retiring after the 1990–91 season.

Hanlon was the last of 10 players to wear No. 1 after Sawchuk's departure in 1964. No. 1 was taken out of circulation until it was officially retired in March 1994.

14 Who says you can't get much for a buck? The Red Wings got a four-time Stanley Cup-winning center for a measly one-dollar bill.

Kris Draper had been a third-round pick (No. 62) by the Winnipeg Jets in the 1989 NHL Draft, but hadn't been able to stick while playing pieces of three seasons with the Jets from 1990–93. He had three points, all goals, in 20 games and spent most of that time with the Moncton Hawks of the American Hockey League.

But proving that one team's trash is another team's treasure, the Red Wings saw something in Draper the Jets hadn't. On June 30, 1993, the Wings acquired him from the Jets for what were called "future considerations," something that actually proved to be worth less than the price of a cup of coffee.

Not in their wildest dreams could the Red Wings have hoped to get a player who would play for them for the next 17 seasons and become a regular on four championship teams.

Draper became a fixture on what became known as the "Grind Line," skating between Darren McCarty and Joe Kocur (later Kirk Maltby) on a ferocious checking unit that did a lot of the dirty work

Kris Draper became a four-time Stanley Cup winner with the Red Wings. (By Dan4th Nicholas—080202 red wings at bruins (369), License: CC BY 2.0, Source: https://commons.wikimedia.org/w/index.php?curid=4833774)

that title-winning teams need. Perhaps their best work came in the 1997 Stanley Cup Final, when the trio of Draper, McCarty, and Maltby shut down the Philadelphia Flyers' "Legion of Doom" line during Detroit's four-game sweep. With the Grind Line doing most of the heavy lifting, the Red Wings limited 50-goal scorer John LeClair to two goals and star center Eric Lindros to one (he scored with 15 seconds left in Game 4).

"It was such a huge honor and a huge thrill for us to be able to be put in those situations," Draper told NHL.com in 2013. "Whether you're playing against Lindros, playing against [Peter] Forsberg or [Joe] Sakic, or playing against [Mike] Modano, we took a lot of pride in that. We also felt that we could chip in with some goals offensively. That was something we were able to do.

"We were going to play. We were going to play hard. We were going to compete and felt that we could do some good things."

Draper even became an offensive contributor, although it's somewhat ironic that his best offensive season, 2003–04, with career highs of 24 goals and 40 points, ended with him being recognized with the Selke Trophy, an award given to the NHL's best *defensive* forward.

Draper was still contributing in 2008, when he helped the Red Wings win the Cup for the fourth time in 12 years. He retired after the 2010–11 season, having played 1,137 games with the Red Wings and contributing 361 points (158 goals, 203 assists).

That's a lot of bang for a buck!

A few months after the Red Wings won the Cup in 1997, Draper gave owner Mike Ilitch and his wife, Marian, a personal token of his appreciation.

"I was able to give Mr. and Mrs. Ilitch the dollar back, so I'd like to think that we're even," Draper told NHL.com. "Who would have thought that number one, a player was going to be traded for a dollar, and then certainly I'm real proud of everything that went on and all the proud moments I had within the organization."

15 It seems so logical now, but it took a Hall of Fame coach, Scotty Bowman, to put the Red Wings' five Russian players together on the ice at the same time.

Actually, what Bowman did was pretty much standard operating procedure back in Russia, going back to the days of the Soviet Union, when five-man units were common. That practice was almost unheard of in North America, where forward lines were, and generally still are, mixed with different defensive pairings.

On October 26, 1995, the "Russian Five" quintet of forwards Sergei Fedorov, Igor Larionov, and Vyacheslav Kozlov and defensemen Vladimir Konstantinov and Viacheslav Fetisov made its debut against the Calgary Flames and helped the Red Wings score two of their three goals—one each by Kozlov and Larionov—in a 3–0 victory.

"My main trick was not to unite all five Russians every time," Bowman told NHL.com in 2015. "I was worried that the opponents would be able to figure out how to play against them. Often, I would wait until the second or even third period to get them out on the ice together. It always got other teams confused."

The Red Wings already had Fedorov, Kozlov, and the two defensemen when they made what seemed to be an odd trade early in the 1995–96 season, sending right wing Ray Sheppard, who had scored 150 goals for Detroit in the previous four seasons, to the San Jose Sharks for Larionov, then 34. Though Larionov had been a star in the USSR, he hadn't put up big scoring numbers after being allowed to come to the NHL and joining the Vancouver Canucks in 1989.

But Bowman knew what he was doing.

"At that time, we had too many right wings," Bowman said. "The Sharks gave me a massive list of players to choose from in exchange for Sheppard. I wasn't looking for a center, but when I saw Larionov's name, I thought that it would be great to get a player with such enormous hockey IQ and put all five Russian guys together."

Larionov's nickname, "The Professor," was an indicator that he had the hockey IQ Bowman was looking for.

The Russian Five didn't play the dump-and-chase style that most NHL teams used. They relied on their speed and puck control. The wings, Fedorov (who switched from center when Larionov arrived) and Kozlov, would often switch sides. That helped create more scoring chances, because many opponents didn't know how to play against them.

"I remember Larionov and his linemates always saying that if you have the puck, you control the game," Ken Holland, then Detroit's assistant general manager, told NHL.com. "They came from the same school of hockey and shared a similar mentality. They understood each other perfectly."

Each of the five Russians added something special. Fedorov, who in 1994 had become the first player born in Europe to win the Hart Trophy, had dazzling speed and skill, making him a threat to score any time he was on the ice. Kozlov was a terrific passer with a big slap shot. Larionov was one of the great playmakers in hockey history, Konstantinov provided a physical element and solid defensive play, and while

Fetisov was no longer the world's best defenseman, he was still terrific in his own zone and had excellent offensive skills.

With the five Russians playing mostly as one unit, the Red Wings set an NHL record for victories in 1995–96 by winning 62 games. In 1996–97, they were a key to Detroit's first Stanley Cup championship since 1955.

"When the Russian Five were on the ice, you had to have your popcorn ready, because you knew that you were in for a treat," Bowman said. "They didn't just play hockey, they created masterpieces on the ice."

Pavel Datsyuk came along after the "Russian Five" era. The Red Wings selected him in the sixth round (No. 151) of the 1998 NHL Draft. But they didn't bring him to Detroit until the 2001–02 season, just in time to be part of another Stanley Cup-winning team.

16 After going 42 years without winning the Stanley Cup, the Red Wings won back-to-back titles in 1997 and 1998—and they swept the Final each time. The Red Wings were a definite underdog as they prepared for the first game of the 1997 Stanley Cup Final against the Philadelphia Flyers. The 1996–97 team had plummeted from 131 points in 1995–96 to 94 and a second-place finish in the Central Division behind the Dallas Stars.

But the first three rounds of the playoffs were another story. After losing, 2–0, in the opener of their Western Conference Quarterfinal series against the St. Louis Blues, the Wings won four of the next five games. That was followed by a sweep of the Mighty Ducks of Anaheim in the conference semifinals, and a bitterly fought six-game win against the Colorado Avalanche in the conference final just one year after the Avs had defeated them in the same round on their way to winning the 1996 Stanley Cup.

The Flyers breezed through their first three rounds, eliminating the Pittsburgh Penguins, Buffalo Sabres, and New York Rangers in five games apiece behind the "Legion of Doom." The line of center Eric Lindros between left wing John LeClair and right wing Mikael Renberg terrorized opponents with their combination of size and skill.

Lindros, in particular, had excelled against the Rangers, dominating New York's defense and making 36-year-old Mark Messier look his age.

In the run-up to the series opener on May 31 at Core States Center (now Wells Fargo Center), the question was how the Wings would cope with Lindros and his linemates. The Red Wings didn't have the kind of size, especially on defense, they were expected to need.

Still, there's more than one way to ground a Flyer. Instead of trying to match muscle with muscle, coach Scotty Bowman decided to defuse Philadelphia with skill. The pairing of Nicklas Lidstrom and Larry Murphy wasn't going to outmuscle anyone, but their combined skills helped defuse Philadelphia's big line.

The Red Wings stunned the packed house of 20,291 by winning the opener, 4–2. Lindros had two assists, one on a goal by LeClair, but Joe Kocur's unassisted goal late in the series put Detroit ahead to stay. Sergei Fedorov and Steve Yzerman each scored, and Mike Vernon made 26 saves.

Three nights later, the Red Wings quieted a crowd of more than 20,000 with another 4–2 win. Kirk Maltby broke a 2–2 tie in the second period and Brendan Shanahan scored his second goal of the game midway through the third. Vernon was sharp again, making 29 saves.

The crowd of 19,983 that packed Joe Louis Arena for Game 3 on June 5 undoubtedly was thinking of a sweep. LeClair's power-play goal 7:03 into the game dampened the atmosphere, but only briefly. Yzerman tied the game two minutes later, Fedorov and Martin Lapointe made it 3–1 before the end of the period, and the Wings cruised to a 6–1 win and a 3–0 series lead.

Philadelphia played with desperation in Game 4, but the Wings were just too much for them. Lidstrom put Detroit ahead at 19:27 of the first period, and Darren McCarty's goal 3:02 into the second made it 2–0. Vernon was 15 seconds from a shutout in the clincher when Lindros scored his only goal of the series, but it was too little, too late. The 2–1 win gave the Red Wings a sweep and their first Cup in 42 years.

In contrast, the Wings were heavy favorites to keep the Cup in 1998. They had defeated the Phoenix Coyotes, St. Louis Blues, and Dallas Stars in six games each, and their opponent in the Final was the

Washington Capitals, who had finished fourth in the Eastern Conference but got an easy path to the first Stanley Cup Final in franchise history when the two division winners in the East, the Pittsburgh Penguins and New Jersey Devils, were upset in the first round of the playoffs.

The Red Wings won, 2–1, in the opener at Joe Louis Arena. Lidstrom and Kocur scored in the first period. Richard Zednik's second-period goal was the only one of Washington's 17 shots to beat goalie Chris Osgood.

Washington led, 3–1, after two periods in Game 2 and was ahead, 4–2, with less than 12 minutes left in the third period. But goals by Lapointe and Doug Brown forced overtime, and Kris Draper beat Olaf Kolzig at 15:24 of OT for a 5–4 win.

Fedorov's goal at 15:09 of the third period gave the Red Wings a 2–1 win in Game 3, and Brown scored two goals in Detroit's 4–1 win in Game 4, making Detroit the first (and still only) team since the New York Islanders in 1982–83 to sweep the Final in back-to-back years.

17 Following a sweep by the New Jersey Devils in the 1995 Stanley Cup Final and coming up short in 1996 after setting an NHL regular-season record for victories, the Red Wings knew they had to make some changes.

The Wings decided they wanted Brendan Shanahan, a high-scoring power forward who'd had two 50-goal seasons and scored 44 goals for the Hartford Whalers in 1995–96 despite playing with a sore wrist. Shanahan had made it clear he wanted out of Hartford, but future Hall of Famers don't come cheap, and the Whalers weren't going to give him Shanahan away, no matter how much he wanted to leave.

On October 9, 1996, the Red Wings got their man, acquiring Shanahan and defenseman Brian Glynn from the Whalers. But Shanahan didn't come cheap: The Red Wings had to send center Keith Primeau and a first-round draft pick to the Whalers, along with another future Hall of Famer, defenseman Paul Coffey.

Not that Coffey, who had won the Stanley Cup three times with the Edmonton Oilers and one with the Pittsburgh Penguins, was dying to leave Detroit.

Coffey, 37, didn't want to leave a potential Cup-winning team near the end of his stellar career to go to the Whalers. He was benched by coach Scotty Bowman for the Wings' 1996 season opener at New Jersey and paid for his own plane ride home.

Bowman told Mitch Albom of the *Detroit Free Press* that Coffey attempted to negate the deal with two phone calls, one to Primeau, who Coffey instructed to refuse a trade, and a second to Whalers general manager Jim Rutherford, to express his displeasure and reluctance to play in Hartford. Coffey denied the charges.

According to the *Hartford Courant*, Bowman never told Coffey about the trade—the defenseman learned about it from the sad expression of a Wings assistant equipment manager.

"He did some things . . . probably to hurt me or whatever," Coffey said about Bowman to the *Courant*. "He made it as difficult as possible.

"But anybody that has ever known me will say that I don't look to knock people to make myself look better. For me to take shots at anybody would be a very insecure thing, and I'm not like that. It's just not worth it.

"The way this was handled was very disappointing."

Coffey joined the Whalers for the 1996–97 season. But after 20 games, he found himself traded once again—to the Philadelphia Flyers. After stints with the Chicago Blackhawks and the Carolina Hurricanes, Coffey played his final season, 2000–01, with the Boston Bruins. He was inducted into the Hockey Hall of Fame in 2004, and his No. 7 was retired by the Oilers the next year.

Shanahan's arrival proved to be the missing piece. He played nine seasons and 716 games with the Wings, scoring 309 goals and adding 324 assists for 633 points. Shanahan played on the Cup-winning teams in 1997, 1998, and 2002, scoring 22 goals (including six game-winners) and adding 23 assists.

"It was a catalyst for our team," Bowman told the *Edmonton Journal*. "He was a big-game player. In the playoffs, he could get to the stage."

18 Gordie Howe didn't win as many NHL scoring titles as Wayne Gretzky, but not even the Great One managed as many top-five finishes as Mr. Hockey.

From 1949–50, when he was third in the NHL with 68 points, though 1968–69, when he was third again, with 103 points, Howe was never out of the top five.

That 20-season streak began when Howe came in third behind linemates Ted Lindsay (78 points) and Sid Abel (69) in 1949–50, his fourth NHL season. It marked the first time that linemates had finished 1–2–3 in the scoring race.

For the next four seasons, Howe took custody of the Art Ross Trophy. He led the NHL in 1950–51 with 86 points and had the same number with the same result in 1951–52. Howe bumped that total up to 95 points in 1952–53, finishing 24 points ahead of runner-up Lindsay and cruising to his third straight scoring title. He had "only" 81 points in 1953–54, but that was still 14 more than runner-up Maurice Richard of the Montreal Canadiens.

Howe dropped to 62 points in 64 games in 1954–55, falling to fifth in the scoring race. He also failed to lead the Wings in scoring for the first time since 1949–50, finishing four points behind Dutch Reibel.

Howe was back up to 79 points in 1955–56, finishing second in the NHL to Montreal's Jean Beliveau. But he won the Art Ross Trophy again in 1956–57 with 89 points, finishing four ahead of Lindsay.

For the next five seasons, Howe was remarkably consistent. He finished with anywhere from 72 to 78 points and came in fifth (twice), fourth (twice), and third (once) in the scoring race. In 1962–63, Howe was back on top with 86 points, five more than Andy Bathgate of the New York Rangers.

For the final four seasons of the Original Six era, Howe was among the NHL's most consistent scorers, finishing fifth, third, fifth, and fourth. He followed a 65-point season in 1966–67, the last of the six-team NHL, by piling up 82 points in 1967–68, the first season after the NHL expanded to 12 teams. That was good enough for a third-place finish.

With offense on the rise, Howe's 103-point season in 1968–69 was only good for third behind Phil Esposito of the Boston Bruins (126) and Bobby Hull of the Chicago Black Hawks (107). Then again, each was a lot younger than Howe, who turned 41 late in the season.

Howe finally fell out of the top five in 1969–70, when he finished with 71 points (31 goals, 40 assists) in 76 games. But though he finished ninth in the scoring race, he was still voted an NHL First-Team All-Star for the final time.

Injuries finally caught up to Howe in 1970–71, his final season with the Red Wings, when he had 23 goals and 52 points in 63 games. He retired from the Red Wings after that, only to return to hockey in 1973 with Houston of the World Hockey Association.

19 Gordie Howe scored 786 goals during his Hall of Fame career with the Red Wings. He was the first player in NHL history to score 600, 700, and (with the Hartford Whalers in 1979–80) 800 goals.

Four more players—Phil Esposito, Marcel Dionne, Wayne Gretzky, and Mike Gartner—followed Howe into the 700-goal club. Dionne, who played his first four seasons in Detroit, was the only one of the four who had spent any time with the Red Wings.

Then, on February 10, 2003, Brett Hull joined Howe as the only two players who scored their 700th NHL goals with the Red Wings.

Hull, whose father Bobby Hull scored 610 NHL goals, came into the Red Wings' game against the San Jose Sharks at Joe Louis Arena with 699 goals, a number he'd been stuck on for seven games. The drought finally ended at 16:54 of the second period, when Hull took a cross-ice pass from Pavel Datsyuk and one-timed a shot past goaltender Evgeni Nabokov for the milestone goal.

Hull had a big smile on his face as his teammates jumped off the bench to celebrate with him. When asked if his accomplishment had sunk in yet, Hull said, "I think so. It's been seven games, so I think it has."

The goal put Detroit ahead, 3–2, in a game that went back and forth until Patrick Boileau beat Nabokov with a high shot from the right circle for his second NHL goal with 2:37 remaining in the third period to give the Red Wings a 5–4 win.

"I'm only 698 behind," joked Boileau, a journeyman who had spent most of the season with Grand Rapids of the American Hockey League.

That victory ended a six-game winless streak for the Red Wings and left Hull in an even happier mood.

"It's big that we won," Hull said. "The last thing I wanted to do was get this goal down 4–0. I wanted it to be in a win."

20 What could be better than having a future Hockey Hall of Famer like Nicklas Lidstrom on defense? How about a Hall of Fame partner?

No one realized it at the time, but that's what ultimately happened when the Red Wings acquired Larry Murphy from the Toronto Maple Leafs on March 18, 1997.

Murphy, an excellent puck mover, had helped the Pittsburgh Penguins win the Stanley Cup in 1991 and 1992. The Toronto Maple Leafs thought he'd be a great addition to their team when they acquired him from the Penguins in July 1995; Murphy was coming off a season in which he'd been named an NHL Second-Team All-Star and finished fourth in balloting for the Norris Trophy.

But Murphy and the Maple Leafs weren't exactly a match made in hockey heaven. After a third-place finish in the Central Division and a first-round loss in the playoffs in 1995–96, the Leafs fell apart in 1996–97—and Murphy took a lot of the blame. The boos rained down on a nightly basis at Maple Leaf Gardens, and Murphy took plenty of heat as the team plummeted to the bottom of the division.

By trade deadline time, the Leafs were looking to cut their losses. Meanwhile, the Red Wings wanted another defenseman who could move the puck and take some of the load off Lidstrom. That man was Murphy, who came to Detroit for the ever-popular "future considerations."

One big reason Murphy wound up in Hockeytown was that Scotty Bowman, who had coached him in Pittsburgh, pushed for the deal. The reunion revitalized Murphy's career.

"I had a great experience with Scotty in Pittsburgh. That was a big factor," Murphy told NHL.com in 2011. "I believed the team had a great chance to win the Cup, because Scotty was the coach. I knew what to expect going into it."

Murphy had six points (two goals, four assists) for the Wings in the regular season after the trade. But he hit his stride in the postseason, leading all Detroit defensemen with 11 points and topping all players with a plus-16 rating.

It didn't happen right away, but the combination of Murphy and Lidstrom made beautiful music together.

"For a time there, Scotty had me playing with [center] Sergei Fedorov as my partner after he moved him back to defense," Murphy told NHL.com. "When he moved Sergei back to forward, he put me with Nick. At that time, I had heard about what a good player Nick Lidstrom was, but at that point in his career he wasn't as well-known as he is now. It didn't take very long to see what a great player he was. I was very fortunate to have him as a partner. He was probably the easiest partner I ever played with, because he was so reliable and so dependable. You just knew where he was going to be, and you could always count on him."

With Lidstrom and Murphy as their top defensive pair, the Red Wings rolled to the Cup in 1997, sweeping the Philadelphia Flyers in the Final.

Murphy had 11 goals and 52 points for Detroit in 1997–98 and was plus-35. The Red Wings won the Cup again in 1998.

Murphy spent most of his time in Detroit as Lidstrom's partner before retiring in 2001. The two are together now in the Hockey Hall of Fame.

"For me, it was a tremendous opportunity playing with a guy like that," Murphy told MLive.com in 2012. "Reliable, Mr. Consistent, he was the perfect defense partner. . . . People that know the game know just how great he was. He wasn't a guy that was out there for the flash, he wasn't putting a show on for anybody, he was just going out there and getting the job done."

21 Detroit was the center of automobile production in the United

States after World War II, so when the Red Wings' new coach, Tommy Ivan, replaced Jack Adams in 1947 and put two youngsters, left wing Ted Lindsay and right wing Gordie Howe, on the flanks with veteran center Sid Abel, "The Production Line" was born.

Abel was nearing the end of a career that would see him earn induction into the Hockey Hall of Fame. But Ivan felt putting him with a pair of younger, faster wings would provide a perfect blend of speed, skill and smarts.

How right he turned out to be!

In an era when goalies almost never came out of their crease to play the puck, the Red Wings adopted the strategy of having Howe and Lindsay dump the puck into the zone and angle it so the other one would be able to play the carom. (This worked especially well at the Olympia, where the home-ice advantage included very lively boards that were angled so that dump-ins usually kicked out toward the slot.)

The threesome led the Wings in scoring in 1947–48 and helped the Red Wings advance to the Stanley Cup Final, although they lost to the Toronto Maple Leafs. By 1949–50, they were 1–2–3 in the NHL in scoring—a feat that has never been repeated—and this time they powered the Red Wings to the Cup.

The trio's success brought the need for a catchy nickname. "The Production Line" captured their scoring prowess as well as referencing the city where the Red Wings played.

The original "Production Line" stayed together until Abel was traded in 1952, but when Alex Delvecchio took over in the middle, "Production Line II" continued to make life miserable for opposing defenses. The latter trio stayed together until Lindsay was traded to Chicago after the 1956–57 season.

22 It's hard to picture a hockey player who was all of 5-foot-8 and 165 pounds earning the nickname "Terrible Ted." Then again, Ted Lindsay was no ordinary player.

Lindsay was a fascinating combination of talents, at once a skilled scorer who was the left wing on a team that won the Stanley Cup four times in six seasons, but also a player who would fight, could hold his own in the corners and spent more time in the penalty box than any star player of his generation.

"I hated everybody. I had no friends," Lindsay told NHL.com in 2016 when asked about his ferocious approach to the game. "I wasn't there to make friends. I was there to win. It wasn't necessary that I score, but I figured I could be an integral part without scoring. I had ability, I had talent, and I didn't have an ego that I thought I was great. I realized I had to earn it. That was my purpose—to be the best that there was at the left-wing position.

"I never looked at stats. I was part of a team. I couldn't do it by myself and nobody else on the team could do it themselves. We were part of a team. I had to help my teammates as much as they helped me. That was my philosophy."

Lindsay loved you if you wore the same jersey he did. If not. . .

"My hatred was sincere," he said. "I liked to see [my opponents] dead. That was my problem, I guess. I understood people, understood human nature. I wasn't a psychologist or anything, but I knew people. You'd figure out who the chickens were on the other side, who the bulls were on the other side, [then] spend your time with the chickens and stay away from the bulls."

The rivalries between the Original Six teams were real. Teams played each other 12, and later 14, times per season, often home-and-home on Saturday and Sunday. There was no players union, no fraternization among opposing players. Players who fought one night often saw each other again 24 hours later.

"You never had to get him that night, that month, even that season," Lindsay told NHL.com of avenging a slight from an opponent. "If he got you dirty . . . I never got people dirty, [but] I'd get ya.

"I never would purposely try to injure anybody. But I'd purposely try to get you out of the game if I could . . . intimidate you. *When Lindsay comes on the ice, where is he?* That's the way I wanted him to think. When I came on the ice, *Where the hell is he?*

"I loved the corners. That's where you found men. You found more chickens. You knew who the chickens were on the other team, because they'd always back off a little bit. If I was coming, they knew they were going to get lumber or elbows or anything. They were going to get into the screen [before there was glass]."

Toronto newspapers nicknamed him "Terrible Ted," and, later, "Scarface." That never bothered him.

"I was there to win," he said. "If it meant taking you to the boards or whatever it was, intimidation would be the best way to do it.

"Everything was fun. I couldn't wait until the next game. Some nights I was so good, but some nights I was so bad, I couldn't wait until the next game to prove I wasn't that bad. It was personal within me, I didn't talk to anybody about it. I knew what my capabilities were. I didn't need a coach to get me up, I was up for everybody."

The funny thing was that away from the ice, Lindsay was anything but terrible. He has raised millions of dollars for charities and is beloved within hockey circles and around the Detroit area.

"I represent my family, my mom and dad," he told NHL.com. "They gave me a proper upbringing, and I've tried to follow that all my life. I've kept my nose clean, as much as I could." He laughed, the interviewer said, and added, "Away from the ice."

23 Billy Smith of the New York Islanders was the first NHL goaltender to be credited with scoring a goal. Smith made a save during a delayed penalty against the Colorado Rockies on November 28, 1979. Colorado defenseman Rob Ramage picked up the rebound and backpassed it into his own net. Smith, the last player to touch the puck, was credited with the goal.

Ron Hextall of the Philadelphia Flyers became the first goaltender to score a goal by shooting the puck into the net when he scaled the puck into an empty net against the Boston Bruins on December 8, 1987. Hextall also became the first NHL goaltender to score a goal during a Stanley Cup Playoff game, when he shot the puck into the empty net against the Washington Capitals on April 11, 1989.

No goaltender scored again until March 6, 1996, when Chris Osgood of the Red Wings did it against the Hartford Whalers.

Like Hextall, Osgood did the deed himself. With time running out and the Red Wings leading, 3–2, at the Hartford Civic Center, Osgood corralled a shot and, instead of putting the puck behind the net or into the corner, dropped it to the ice. In one quick move, he took a shot up the middle of the ice. No Whaler came close to touching the puck (though a teammate nearly got hit in the face) before it nestled into the net, wrapping up a 4–2 victory

"It was great, I was really excited," Osgood said after his league-leading 32nd victory. "In juniors, I used to take shots all the time, but here I usually pass it off to a defenseman. When we got the empty net this time, I said I was going to go for it."

Said Red Wings coach Scotty Bowman, "I've never seen that play live in all my years. I have never had it happen to me in nearly 2,000 games."

Osgood did more than just score a goal that season. He had one of the greatest seasons by a goaltender in NHL history, going 39–6–5 with a 2.11 goals-against average for a Detroit team that finished with 62 victories and finished first in the overall standings.

Though it was Osgood's first and only NHL goal, it wasn't the first one he'd ever scored in a game. While playing in juniors with Medicine Hat of the Western Hockey League, Osgood scored a goal on January 3, 1991.

24 The Red Wings were a dynasty in the early 1950s and one of the NHL's most consistent teams through the 1960s, then hit the skids in the 1970s and early 1980s. They qualified for the Stanley Cup Playoffs once from 1971 to 1983 and finished above .500 only once during that span.

It's easy to forget now that, in those days, the Red Wings were a mess on and off the ice. The nickname "Dead Things" had become attached to the Wings, whose season ticket base in the new, 20,000-seat Joe Louis Arena was down to about 2,100.

Happily for those fans who remained, Mike Ilitch came along.

Ilitch had played minor-league baseball before his hopes for a big-league career were derailed by a knee injury. He went into the pizza

Joe Louis Arena was the home of the Red Wings from December 1979 to April 2017. (Schmackity [GFDL (http://www.gnu.org/copyleft/fdl.html) or License: CC-BY-SA-3.0; Source: http://creativecommons.org/licenses/by-sa/3.0/], from Wikimedia Commons)

business in the Detroit area and thrived; eventually, his Little Caesars chain became one of the biggest in the country.

But Ilitch never lost his love for sports, or for Detroit. On June 3, 1982, he combined the two when he and his wife, Marian, bought the Red Wings from Bruce Norris, whose family had run the team for 50 years. *The New York Times* estimated the price at $10 million to $12 million. Later reports pegged it at $8 or $9 million.

Success was anything but immediate. The Red Wings missed the playoffs in 1982–83 and were 18th in the 21-team league. But the first big on-ice piece of the team's transformation came in June 1983, when the Red Wings selected center Steve Yzerman with the fourth pick in the NHL draft.

It took some time, but by the late 1980s, general manager Jim Devellano, one of the key members of the front office that built the New York Islanders' dynasty in the 1980s, was beginning to put the pieces of one of the NHL's great teams in place.

Unlike his business interests, Ilitch ran the Red Wings with the pure goal of winning championships. If that meant overspending, so be it. He believed in hiring good people and letting them do their jobs. The payoff was four Stanley Cup championships from 1996–97 through 2007–08, a 25-season run of Stanley Cup Playoff berths—and sellout crowds at The Joe and the new Little Caesars Arena.

In 2006, Kevin Allen and Art Regner teamed to write a book about Red Wings history, *What it Means to Be a Red Wing*. The Ilitches wrote the introduction, which concluded:

> *If you ask us what it means to be a Red Wing, we would say it means that everyone in the organization strives for success while conducting himself, or herself, in a classy and professional manner. It's about pride. Little Caesars is a family business. And the Detroit Red Wings are a family organization. Pride has played an important role in the success of each venture.*

25 The Red Wings hadn't been good for a long time when Mike and Marian Ilitch bought the team from Bruce Norris, whose family had owned the franchise for a half-century. The organization was a mess. Coaches and general managers had come and gone for more than a decade, but while the names changed, the results were largely the same.

Luckily for the Red Wings, the Ilitches found the right man to resurrect the team.

Jim Devellano was Bill Torrey's right-hand man with the New York Islanders, helping to turn a team that set NHL records for futility in 1972–73, its first NHL season, into a dynasty that won the Stanley Cup four straight times from 1980 to 1983.

But Devellano wasn't there for the last Cup. He was the first person hired after the Ilitches bought the team. The 2018–19 season is his

37th with the Wings; according to the team, he's the longest-serving hockey employee in the franchise's 90-plus years in the NHL.

Devellano, a Toronto native, hadn't played pro hockey. But he'd become a scout with the St. Louis Blues in 1967, when the NHL expanded from six to 12 teams. He joined the Islanders when they were added to the NHL in 1972 and scouted most of the players who became the core of one of the greatest dynasties in any sport. He also urged GM Bill Torrey to hire one of his former players in St. Louis, Al Arbour, as coach after that dreadful first season. Arbour coached the Islanders to all four championships.

In 1979–80, Devellano became general manager of the Islanders' Indianapolis farm club in the Central Hockey League and was named Minor League Executive of the Year by *The Hockey News*. He returned to New York in 1981 as the Islanders' assistant general manager.

That resume was more than enough to attract the interest of the Ilitches. He was hired as general manager and served in that capacity for eight seasons before being named senior vice president in 1990.

Devellano was one of the first NHL general managers to assemble a strong European scouting staff, a move that produced several Red Wings standouts, including Russians Sergei Fedorov, Slava Kozlov, Vladimir Konstantinov, and Pavel Datsyuk, as well as Swedes Nicklas Lidstrom, Tomas Holmstrom, Henrik Zetterberg, Johan Franzen, and Niklas Kronwall.

During Devellano's tenure, the Red Wings have participated in 10 conference finals (1987–88, 1995–98, 2002, and 2007–09) and six Stanley Cup Finals (1995, '97, '98, '02, '08, and 2009), winning four. They won the Presidents' Trophy six times (1995, '96, 2002, '04, '06, and 2008), took home the regular-season Western Conference championship eight times (1994-96, 2002, '04, and 2006–08), and won 16 division championships (1988–89, '92, 1994–96, '99, 2001–04, 2006–09, and 2011).

Devellano received the Lester Patrick Award for his outstanding service to the sport of hockey in the United States in October 2009. He was inducted into the Hockey Hall of Fame in the Builder Category on November 8, 2010.

26 The Red Wings have had a variety of farm teams, beginning with the Detroit Olympics of the International Hockey League in 1932. Those teams have ranged from the East Coast (Baltimore Clippers of the American Hockey League), to the West Coast (San Diego Gulls of the Western Hockey League), and plenty of places in between.

Most of the affiliations lasted just a few years, though some had multiple stints. Others, like the current affiliation with the Grand Rapids Griffins of the AHL, have lasted well over a decade. But the longest-tenured affiliation came with one of the smallest market teams: The Adirondack Red Wings, based in Glens Falls, New York, from 1979 to 1999.

Ned Harkness, the former coach and general manager of the Red Wings, had become the director of the new Glens Falls Civic Center and persuaded owner Bruce Norris to move the Wings' primary development team from Kansas City of the Central Hockey League to Glens Falls, where there was an AHL team that became known as the Adirondack Red Wings.

The new affiliate dressed like the parent team and was a hit from the start, routinely packing the Civic Center. On-ice success came quickly. Led by longtime NHL star Peter Mahovlich, Adirondack won the Calder Cup (the AHL version of the Stanley Cup) in 1980–81, just their second season in Glens Falls, and took home three more titles in the following 11 seasons.

Player turnover is a given in the minors, but Adirondack had less than most teams. More than 30 players played 200 or more games, nine played 300 or more, and two—forward Glenn Merkosky and defenseman Greg Joly—dressed for more than 400. That kind of stability helped Adirondack make the Calder Cup playoffs in 19 of their 20 seasons.

Hall of Famer Adam Oates spent time in Adirondack. Neil Smith, who went on to build the team that ended the New York Rangers' 54-year Stanley Cup drought in 1994, was Adirondack's GM before being hired by New York in 1989.

By the late 1990s, the Red Wings began looking to bring their AHL team closer to Detroit. The Red Wings shared the Cincinnati Mighty Ducks with Anaheim from 1999 to 2002 before getting their own AHL team in Grand Rapids in 2002. The franchise that was Adirondack went dormant until 2002, when it was purchased by the NBA's San Antonio Spurs. The San Antonio Rampage will serve as the St. Louis Blues' AHL team beginning in 2018–19.

27 Jeff Blashill never saw the ice in the NHL after playing three seasons in the USHL and four at Ferris State University. But he wasted little time getting into coaching and was named as the Red Wings' new bench boss on June 9, 2015, after Mike Babcock left to take over the Toronto Maple Leafs.

Though he was just 41 when he took over the Red Wings, Blashill didn't lack for experience. One year after finishing his playing career, Blashill returned to his alma mater as an assistant coach. Three seasons later, he moved on to Miami University in Ohio, where he spent six more seasons as an assistant.

Blashill got his first chance to run a team in 2008–09, when he took over the Indiana Ice of the USHL. He led Indiana to a 39–19–2 record in his first season, and the Ice went on to win the league championship. They were 33–24–3 in his second season, but lost in the second round of the playoffs.

The next step was Western Michigan, where he led the Broncos to a 19–13–10 record in 2010–11. That turned out to be his one and only season at WMU. The Red Wings hired him as an assistant under Babcock in July 2011.

Blashill spent one season as an assistant in Detroit before taking over as coach of the Red Wings' AHL farm team, the Grand Rapids Griffins. He got the job when Curt Fraser left to become an assistant with the Dallas Stars.

As he had done at Indiana, Blashill coached his new team to a title in his first season. The Griffins won the Calder Cup in 2013, the first AHL title in the franchise's history. The Griffins were 88–48–2–12 in their next two seasons, and Blashill was named the AHL's outstanding coach in 2014–15. When Babcock left to go to the Maple Leafs, Detroit GM Ken Holland wasted little time promoting Blashill to replace him.

28 Anthony Mantha had everything the Red Wings could have asked for when they selected him in the first round (No. 20) of the 2013 NHL Draft—including good hockey genes.

Mantha, a native of Longueuil, Quebec, scored 50 goals for Val-d'Or of the Quebec Major Junior Hockey League in his draft season, then bumped that total to 57 in 2013–14. But an ankle injury sustained in training camp derailed his hopes of making the Red Wings right away, and he spent all of the 2014–15 season and most of 2015–16 with Detroit's AHL affiliate, the Grand Rapids Griffins.

Mantha got his first taste of the NHL during a late-season call-up, and he scored his first NHL goal on March 25, 2016, when he followed the rebound of a shot by Brad Richards and shoveled the puck past Canadiens goalie Ben Scrivens for a goal he'll never forget. His proud grandfather, Andre Pronovost, was on hand at Joe Louis Arena.

Pronovost was a left wing who had helped the Montreal Canadiens win the Stanley Cup four times in a row from 1957 to 1960. He later played three seasons with the Red Wings.

He was caught on camera with a tear in his eye as Mantha's family celebrated Anthony's first NHL goal, one that, ironically, came against the Canadiens.

"It's unbelievable," Mantha said, after his goal turned out to be the game-winner in a 4–3 victory. "Obviously, my grandparents were very happy, my parents also. My friends were probably jumping. One of my buddies told me he was going to go around the rink screaming if I scored."

Pronovost was among the people Mantha had phoned 11 days earlier, when he'd found out he was joining the Red Wings.

"I called him the day I got called up but haven't talked to him since," Mantha told the *Detroit Free Press.*

Even better was to score his first NHL goal against the team his grandfather had played for and that Mantha rooted for as a boy.

"That was my club growing up, my hometown, where I grew up," Mantha said of Montreal, "My grandfather brought me to games there."

29 Gustav Nyquist's road to the NHL started in Sweden, where he played for the Malmo Redhawks organization all the way through 2007–08. But it's here his story takes a twist.

In addition to his hockey skills, Nyquist was also a top student in high school. The Red Wings had drafted him in the fourth round (No. 121) of the 2008 NHL Draft, but Nyquist came to North America and enrolled at the University of Maine.

Nyquist was the top scorer for the Black Bears in each of his three seasons. In 2009–10, he led all of NCAA Division I in scoring with 61 points (19 goals, 42 assists) and was a finalist for the Hobey Baker Award, given to the top player in Division I. After putting up 51 points (18 goals, 33 assists) in 2010–11, he signed a two-year, entry-level contract with the Red Wings.

Nyquist spent most of his first full pro season with Grand Rapids, the Wings' affiliate in the American Hockey League, before making his NHL debut against the Minnesota Wild on November 1, 2011. He scored his first NHL goal on March 26, 2012, against the Columbus Blue Jackets.

Nyquist spent most of 2012–13 with Grand Rapids, largely because of the lockout that reduced the NHL season to 48 games. He had 60 points (23 goals, 37 assists) for Grand Rapids during the regular season, then contributed seven points (two goals, five assists) to the Griffins' run to the Calder Cup championship.

It took until the 2013–14 season for Nyquist to earn a full-time job with the Red Wings. After putting up 21 points (seven goals, 14 assists) in 15 games for Grand Rapids, he became a full-time Wing and led Detroit with 28 goals, despite playing just 57 games. On July 10, 2015, he signed a four-year contract with the Wings. A 27-goal, 54-point season followed in 2014–15, before he had 17 in 2015–16, 12 goals (but 36 assists and 48 points) in 2016–17, and 21 goals in 2017–18.

30 Henrik Zetterberg was determined to remain with the Red Wings, the team that had taken him in the seventh round (No. 210) of the 1999 NHL Draft. With the Wings, he'd become an NHL star, winning the Conn Smythe Trophy as playoff MVP when the Red Wings won the Stanley Cup in 2008.

Zetterberg entered the final season of his contract in 2008–09, but midway through the season, the Red Wings acted to make sure he'd be in Detroit throughout his NHL career. On January 28, 2009, the Red Wings announced that Zetterberg had come to terms on a 12-year contract worth $73 million that would keep him in red and white through the 2020–21 season.

The length of the contract enabled the Red Wings to keep Zetterberg's salary cap hit to a manageable $6.08 million through the contract's term. According to media reports, he made between $7 million and $7.75 million through the first nine seasons of the contract. That was scheduled to drop to $3.5 million in 2018–19 and $1 million in each of the final two seasons, although Zetterberg announced in September 2018 that he would be unable to continue to play hockey because of a degenerative back issue.

"I have never seen any reason to want to go anywhere else," Zetterberg said at the press conference after the signing. "I really like it here, on the ice and off the ice, great teammates, great coaching staff, great owners that know we'll have a good team every year. I don't see any reason why I shouldn't stay. I love it here and I want to be here forever."

General manager Ken Holland was delighted to have Zetterberg locked up long-term for a reasonable cap hit (although the kind of contract he signed would be outlawed in the Collective Bargaining Agreement of 2013).

"Obviously when you talk about a 12-year contract, one of the things obviously is risk, on both sides, and we feel that we were able to find a solution that, there's always risks on both sides, but both sides are very, very excited," Holland said. "And I'm excited that Henrik is going to be a Red Wing for life and a player to build around."

A story in a Swedish newspaper before the 2017–18 season said Zetterberg intended to play just two more seasons. But he wasted no time clarifying that he intended to play for the Wings as long as possible, although that turned out to be just one more season.

Henrik Zetterberg was another find by European scout Christer Rockstrom. (No machine-readable author provided. JamesTeterenko assumed (based on copyright claims). [GFDL (http://www.gnu.org/copyleft/fdl.html) or CC-BY-SA-3.0 (http://creativecommons.org/licenses/by-sa/3.0/)], via Wikimedia Commons)

"I want to play hockey as long as I can," Zetterberg said. "The thing that'll decide if I'm not going to play is my body. If I'm not healthy enough to play, I won't play. But it's [his health, primarily his back that's] been getting better the last couple of years, and hopefully it'll continue that way.

31 The Red Wings' problems in the 1980s had nothing to do with an inability to score; Detroit could fill the net. The problem was that the opposition could do the same, and then some.

The situation improved in the early 1990s under Bryan Murray, but it wasn't until Scotty Bowman was hired as coach for the 1993–94 season that things really began to tighten up.

Bowman had already won the Stanley Cup six times, five with the Montreal Canadiens in the 1970s and again with the Pittsburgh Penguins in 1992. Bowman-coached teams were always good defensively, and he quickly made sure the Red Wings followed suit.

One of the strategies that came to symbolize Bowman's Red Wings was the "left-wing lock."

It's a two-step strategy that's designed to force turnovers and keep opponents from breaking out of their zone quickly. The attacking team dumps the puck deep into the opponent's zone, and the right wing comes in on the forecheck with the objective of forcing the defending team to move the puck the other way. The center, also on the forecheck, tries to force the defending team to move the puck along the boards rather than up the slot or across it. The left wing, who plays higher in the zone, waits along the boards with the defenseman on that side and anticipates causing a turnover.

The left-wing lock works when then puck winds up along the boards on the desired side—ideally the left side, hence the term—and the attacking team can get a manpower advantage in its pursuit of the puck.

The strategy took advantage of the fact that most players shoot left-handed. The attacking team wants to stack the boards with lefty shooters, who, ideally, will outnumber the opponent's number of right-hand shooters.

In a perfect world, the attacking team wins a scrum for the puck, then has some options.

The puck can squirt into the slot for the center to get off a shot. If it stays along the left boards or in the corner, the attacking team can wear down the team playing defense—and a mistake can turn into a scoring opportunity. If the attacking team makes a mistake, on the other hand, usually the worst thing that can happen is that the puck comes out of the zone.

It's a relative of the neutral-zone trap. Each relies on forcing the opposition into an uncomfortable spot with the puck and denying options.

So why don't we see the lock much today?

The best way to beat it (or any trapping system) is with mobile defensemen who can break the puck out of their zone. NHL teams today generally have much more mobility on the blue line and can move the puck quickly before the forecheck can get set up.

32 While Scotty Bowman was coaching the Red Wings to their third Stanley Cup in six seasons in 2002, the Mighty Ducks of Anaheim were looking for a new coach. The found him in Mike Babcock, who had led the Cincinnati Mighty Ducks of the American Hockey League for two seasons, getting them into the Calder Cup playoffs each time.

Babcock, who had played at McGill University, started his coaching career with three seasons at Red Deer College, then spent two

The Red Wings won the Stanley Cup for the fourth time in twelve seasons by defeating the Pittsburgh Penguins in the 2008 Final. (Tom Gromak—Flickr: BB5D5817.jpg, License: CC BY-SA 2.0; Source: https://commons.wikimedia. org/w/index.php?curid=24118512)

seasons coaching Moose Jaw, one at the University of Lethbridge, and six with Spokane of the WHL before going to Cincinnati. (Although Cincinnati took Anaheim's nickname, the Red Wings also used it as their top farm team.)

Babcock got the Mighty Ducks into the Stanley Cup Playoffs his first season in Anaheim, and their first-round playoff opponent was none other than the defending champion Red Wings. But not only did the Mighty Ducks upset them, they swept the series. Detroit had led the NHL in goals during the regular season with 269, but the Red Wings managed just six in the four games and were stymied time and again by goaltender Jean-Sebastien Giguere, who made 165 saves on 171 shots for a .976 save percentage.

The Mighty Ducks then stunned the Dallas Stars in six games in the second round and swept the Minnesota Wild in the Western Conference Final. They got to Game 7 of the Stanley Cup Final before losing to the New Jersey Devils, and despite the loss, Giguere's brilliance earned him the Conn Smythe Trophy as playoff MVP.

The Mighty Ducks struggled in 2003–04, missing the playoffs, and the 2004–05 lockout wiped out what would have been the final season of Babcock's three-year contract.

Babcock declined an offer to remain with Anaheim and was named coach of the Red Wings on July 15, 2005.

It turned out to be a marriage made in hockey heaven. With Babcock behind the bench, the Red Wings remained among the NHL's elite teams for most of the next decade, winning the Stanley Cup again in 2008 and suffering a 2–1 loss to the Pittsburgh Penguins in Game 7 of the 2009 Final.

33 A 3–2 overtime loss to the Columbus Blue Jackets disappointed the crowd of 19,515 who turned out at Little Caesars Arena on October 4, 2018, but it did extend the Red Wings' streak of not losing a home opener in regulation to six.

On October 5, 2017, the Red Wings christened their new home by defeating the Minnesota Wild, 4–2. Anthony Mantha's power-play goal at 14:40 in the second period was the first ever scored in the Red

The Red Wings moved into Little Caesars Arena in October 2017. (Coreyfein01 —Own work, License: CC BY-SA 4.0, Source: https://commons.wikimedia .org/w/index.php?curid=62311810)

Wings' new home, and Henrik Zetterberg's goal 7:07 into the third period broke a tie and proved to be the game-winner. Dylan Larkin and Martin Frk also scored for Detroit, and goaltender Jimmy Howard made 37 saves.

One year earlier, the Wings had begun their final home season at Joe Louis Arena by defeating the Ottawa Senators, 5–1, on October 13, 2016. After losing their first two games of the season on the road at Tampa Bay and Florida, the Red Wings returned home and rolled over the Senators, thanks to the first NHL hat trick by defenseman Mike Green and a 31-save performance by goaltender Petr Mrazek.

The Red Wings started the 2015–16 season at home and blanked the Toronto Maple Leafs, 4–0. It was a rude return to Detroit for longtime Red Wings coach Mike Babcock, whose team couldn't put any of its 22 shots past Howard. Justin Abdelkader had a hat trick for the Red Wings, and Larkin showed off his speed in his NHL debut by scoring one goal and assisting on another.

Howard didn't get a shutout in the 2014–15 season opener at Joe Louis Arena, but he did receive plenty of help from his teammates. Though Patrice Bergeron gave the Boston Bruins an early lead when he scored 12:01 into the game, Abdelkader and Gustav Nyquist had goals in the second period for Detroit, and the Red Wings limited Boston to 17 shots in a 2–1 win. Nyquist's power-play goal at 14:46 of the second period broke a 1–1 tie.

Howard faced seven power plays when the Red Wings opened the 2013–14 season against the Buffalo Sabres at Joe Louis Arena on October 2, 2013, but he had to make just 19 saves in the 2–1 victory. Mikael Samuelsson and Pavel Datsyuk scored in the first period for Detroit, and Howard allowed only a third-period goal by Buffalo's Zemgus Girgensons. The winning margin could have been greater, but Cory Emmerton was unable to score against Sabres goaltender Ryan Miller on a second-period penalty shot.

The last visiting team to spoil the home opener for the Red Wings with a regulation victory was the Dallas Stars, who won, 2–1, on January 22, 2013. It was the first of 24 home games for the Wings during the lockout-shortened 2012–13 season. Howard made 31 saves, but the Red Wings were unable to beat Kari Lehtonen until Datsyuk scored with four seconds remaining in the third period.

34 A New Year's Eve home game is a popular tradition in Detroit. The Red Wings' 4–1 victory over the Pittsburgh Penguins on December 31, 2017, marked the 69th time the Wings have played on New Year's Eve, with 64 of those games at home. The Red Wings haven't played a road game on December 31 since 1956, when they rang out the old year with a 1–0 victory against the New York Rangers at Madison Square Garden.

Gustav Nyquist had two goals for the Red Wings in the win against Detroit, which improved the Red Wings' New Year's Eve game record to 36–24 with eight ties and one shootout loss, including 10–3–0 in the 21st century. It also avenged a 5–2 loss to the Penguins on December 31, 2015, the Red Wings' last New Year's Eve game at Joe Louis Arena (they didn't play on December 31, 2016, because they were playing the Toronto Maple Leafs outdoors in the NHL Centennial Classic on January 1, 2017).

The Red Wings have also done well on Halloween. A 5–3 win against the Arizona Coyotes on October 31, 2017, was their fifth in a row overall on Halloween. Five Red Wings scored and goaltender Jimmy Howard made 30 saves for the win, which gave Detroit a 12–7–0 record with four ties in games played on October 31.

St. Patrick's Day has also been a good day for the Red Wings. Detroit's most recent March 17 game came in 2016, when the Red Wings defeated the Columbus Blue Jackets, 2–1, at Nationwide Arena to improve to 20–14 with one tie and one overtime loss on the holiday. That includes one of the rare forfeit victories in modern NHL history: On March 17, 1955, the Red Wings were leading the Montreal Canadiens, 4–1, after one period at the Forum when a riot broke out. Montreal fans had been enraged after Maurice "Rocket" Richard had been suspended for the remainder of the regular season and the Stanley Cup Playoffs after punching linesman Cliff Thompson during a brawl with Hal Laycoe of the Boston Bruins.

NHL president Clarence Campbell attended the game, but after the Red Wings jumped to an early lead, a tear gas bomb went off and the Forum had to be evacuated, with the Wings winning by forfeit.

Easter is always on a Sunday, but it can come as early as March 22 or as late as April 25, meaning that it can fall late in the regular season or early in the playoffs. The Red Wings haven't played on Easter since losing 2–1 at home to the Washington Capitals in 2015, dropping their overall record on the holiday to 13–16 with three ties. That includes 6–12 with two ties in the regular season and 7–4 with one tie in playoff games.

Detroit's last Easter Sunday win came in 1999, when the Wings blanked the Stars, 3–0, in Dallas. They've lost seven in a row since then.

35 Winning 400 games with the same team is a remarkable achievement for any coach. Through the 2017–18 season, just 34 coaches in NHL history had won 400 or more games in their entire careers, let alone with one team. This is why it's so special that the Red Wings have had three bench bosses with 400-plus wins.

With a little help from the adoption of the shootout, which meant the end of games ending in ties, Mike Babcock piled up 458 victories in just 10 seasons behind the bench in Detroit. Babcock arrived in 2005, the same year the NHL adopted the shootout, and finished his decade with the Wings with a record of 458–273–105 in 786 games. (The 2012–13 season was shortened from 82 to 48 games because of the NHL lockout.)

Babcock's 786 games coached are second in franchise history behind the legendary Jack Adams, whose name adorns the NHL's Coach of the Year award. Adams took over in 1927–28, the second season in the NHL for the team now known as the Red Wings, and stayed behind the bench for 20 seasons, winning 413 games, losing 390 and tying 161 in 964 games.

Scotty Bowman spent the final nine seasons of his Hall of Fame career with the Red Wings, beginning in 1993–94. He got them to the Stanley Cup Final in his second season, coached them to the Cup in 1997, 1998, and 2002, and kept them among the NHL's elite throughout his time in Detroit. Bowman coached 701 games with the Red Wings (a lockout shortened the 1994–95 season to 48 games, and he missed the first five games of the 1998–99 season recovering from surgery), going 410–193 with 88 ties and 10 overtime losses. He stepped down after leading the Red Wings to the Cup in 2002.

Sid Abel is also in the Hockey Hall of Fame, but as a player rather than a coach. Abel, a star center for the Red Wings during his career, took over as coach midway through the 1956–57 season. The Wings went 16–12–5 after he took over and finished third, though they were swept in the Stanley Cup Semifinals.

Abel remained behind the bench through the 1960s, coaching the Red Wings to the Final four times without winning. He stayed behind the bench through the 1969–70 season, when he got the Wings back into the playoffs after a two-season absence.

Abel's 811 regular-season games as coach are second in team history, but he finished 340–339–112, leaving him fourth in victories.

36 Maybe it was appropriate that Steve Yzerman wore No. 19, since he wound up spending 19 seasons as the Red Wings' captain. He was followed by Nicklas Lidstrom, who wore the "C" for six seasons before retiring, then Henrik Zetterberg, who took over after Lidstrom hung up his skates in 2012.

In addition to Yzerman, just one member of the Red Wings served as captain for more than a decade.

Perhaps, surprisingly, it's not Gordie Howe. Mr. Hockey donned the "C" in 1958, after Red Kelly had worn it for two seasons, Ted Lindsay for four, and Sid Abel for seven. Howe served as captain for four seasons, but he gave up the captaincy in the summer of 1962, when Abel, now Detroit's coach, named him as one of his assistants. (The same thing happened with Bobby Clarke and the Philadelphia Flyers a generation later.)

The Red Wings didn't have to look far for a replacement. The "C" moved from right wing to center on the same line when Alex Delvecchio was named captain before the start of the 1962–63 season. He remained captain until the end of his career, in 1973.

Though Howe played more games and played longer, Delvecchio was a career Red Wing. Counting a one-game cup of coffee in 1950–51, he played all or part of 24 seasons with Detroit. No one in pro sports has had a longer career spent with one team than "Fats." His 1,670 games between the regular season and playoffs are the most by anyone who has spent his entire career with one NHL team.

He played with a mixture of skill and grace rarely seen in any sport.

"I think that all records can be broken, and I don't know how much of a record that is, if you even want to call it a record," Delvecchio told Dave Stubbs of NHL.com in 2016. "I guess I was one of the fortunate ones who was able to stay in the League that long. And playing with guys like the late Gordie, and with Ted Lindsay and Red Kelly, that sure helped to keep me in the NHL."

Delvecchio won the Lady Byng Trophy for skillful and gentlemanly play three times; he also finished second or third three times. It wasn't really an award he sought. In Delvecchio's era, GMs around the NHL, including his boss, Jack Adams, prized aggressive play and would grumble that they didn't want Lady Byng winners.

Howe joked in a 1969 *Hockey Illustrated* article that "I don't like to play on the same line as 'Fats.' He is such a smooth skater with that almost delicate toe-dancing style of his that he is worth watching. I can only watch him when he is playing on a different line than I am."

In reality, Howe loved playing with Delvecchio, who assisted on more of his regular-season goals than any other player (210). No one else was close: Lindsay was second with 147.

Delvecchio wore the "C" until he retired early in the 1973–74 season. He remained with the Red Wings as coach from 1974 to 1977, doubling as general manager in an effort to keep the team afloat as the stars of the pre-expansion era faded away and weren't replaced. But he was too much of a gentleman for either job, taking every loss personally.

He retired from the Red Wings organization in 1977, the same year he was inducted into the Hockey Hall of Fame, an honor that reflected his leadership and grace as much as it did the 13 seasons in which he scored 20 or more goals. He had career NHL totals of 456 goals and 1,281 points, plus 35 goals and 104 points in 121 playoff games.

37 The Red Wings have always had a big advantage at home. They had a .636 points percentage at Joe Louis Arena, where they played from late in 1979 through the 2016–17 season, after putting up a .632 percentage at the Olympia from 1927 to 1979.

But the Red Wings didn't get off to a great start at home in 2011–12. After a 4–1 loss to the Calgary Flames at Joe Louis Arena on November 3, 2011, they had an uninspiring 3–2–1 record on their own ice. Little could anyone have known that the loss to the Flames would be the last one at home for more than 3 1/2 months.

Two days after that loss , the Red Wings pummeled the Anaheim Ducks, 5–0, before the usual full house at the Joe. They completed a six-game homestand by defeating the Colorado Avalanche (5–2), the Edmonton Oilers (3–0), and the Dallas Stars (5–2).

After splitting a four-game road trip, the Red Wings got some revenge against the Flames with a 5–3 victory on Thanksgiving Eve. They defeated the Nashville Predators, 4–1, on November 26, then topped the Tampa Bay Lightning, 4–2, four nights later to extend the home winning streak to seven games.

December began with a three-game road trip, but the Red Wings resumed their winning ways at home by defeating the Phoenix Coyotes (5–2) and the Winnipeg Jets (7–1) in their first two home games of the month. Detroit spent most of the rest of the month on the road, but managed to defeat the Los Angeles Kings (8–2 on December 15), St. Louis Blues (3–2 on December 27), and the Blues again (3–0 on New Year's Eve).

That made it 12 in a row, all in regulation, at home. After beginning the new year with a 3–1–0 road trip, it was back to the Joe for three games in a five-day span. All three were wins: 3–2 in overtime against Phoenix, 3–2 in a shootout against the Chicago Blackhawks, and 5–0 against the Buffalo Sabres. The Red Wings won back-to-back shootouts on the road, then made it three in a row in the tiebreaker with a 3–2 victory against the Columbus Blue Jackets on January 21. Two nights later, the Blues fell, 3–1, extending the streak to 17.

The Red Wings returned from the All-Star break with the NHL record for longest home winning streak squarely in their sights; the 1929–30 Boston Bruins and 1975–76 Philadelphia Flyers had each won 20 in a row at home.

After going 2–2–1 during a five-game road trip, the Red Wings returned home for six straight games and picked up where they had left off. Wins against the Oilers, Ducks, and Flyers in a five-day span tied the record, then they broke it on February 14, scoring twice in the first period against the Stars and ending up with a 3–1 win. Joey MacDonald made 20 saves, losing his shutout bid when Adam Burish scored with 33 seconds remaining.

Wins against the Predators (2–1 on February 17) and San Jose Sharks (3–2 on February 19) made it 23 in a row at home and gave the Red Wings an overall record of 41–17–2. They lost, 2–1, at Chicago on the 21st, then came back to the Joe two nights later for a game against the Vancouver Canucks.

It looked like the home winning streak would survive a tough test from the defending Western Conference champions when Justin Abdelkader made it 3–2 with 6:14 remaining in the third period. But the Canucks pulled goaltender Roberto Luongo in the final minute, and Daniel Sedin scored with 16 seconds remaining to send the game into overtime.

The extra five minutes settled nothing, so the teams went to a shootout. The first five shooters came up empty before Vancouver's Alexandre Burrows beat Jimmy Howard for a streak-ending 4–3 win, thus ending the home-game streak at 23.

Two nights later, the Red Wings' point streak at home ended at 24 games with a 4–3 loss to Colorado.

38 The Red Wings had never scored two goals in five seconds until November 24, 2007, when they went to Nationwide Arena for a meeting with the Columbus Blue Jackets.

The crowd of 17,513 roared as the Blue Jackets took a 2–0 lead into the locker room after the first period on goals by Manny Malhotra and Ron Hainsey.

That lead lasted until just past the midway point of the second period, when Tomas Holmstrom got the Wings on the board at 10:44 with a power-play goal, with Pavel Datsyuk and Brian Rafalski getting the assists.

The goal must have stunned the Blue Jackets. Nikolai Zherdev won the ensuing faceoff at center ice, but Datsyuk stole the puck from him, raced in alone, and beat Pascal Leclaire with a rising shot at 10:49. The two goals in five seconds set a franchise record and tied the game, 2–2. However, the game went to a shootout, and all three Columbus shooters beat Wings goalie Chris Osgood for a 3–2 win.

The scenario was the same when the Red Wings matched their record by scoring twice in five seconds in the second period against the Vancouver Canucks on March 20, 2010.

The Wings were desperately trying to scramble their way into a playoff berth in the Western Conference, but they fell behind, 2–0, on first-period goals by Vancouver defensemen Kyle Wellwood and Shane O'Brien.

The Canucks maintained that lead until after the midway point of the middle period. Then, former Canucks forward Todd Bertuzzi got Detroit energized, when he found the puck in the skates of defenseman Kevin Bieksa and poked it past Roberto Luongo at 12:34.

On the ensuing faceoff, Datsyuk won a puck battle, skated across the Vancouver blue line and beat Luongo with a 45-foot wrister past the goaltender's blocker at 12:39. All of a sudden, the game was tied, 2–2.

This one had a happier ending for the Red Wings. Valtteri Filppula made it 3–2 late in the period, and although Daniel Sedin tied the game early in the third period, Henrik Zetterberg beat the clock and the Canucks by lifting a backhander from the slot at 4:59 of overtime for a 4–3 win. It came on Detroit's 54th shot of the game.

39 Steve Yzerman would hold most of the career scoring records for most NHL teams. But the Red Wings aren't just *any* team. They've had some of the greatest scorers in hockey history, most notably Gordie Howe.

Howe played the last of his 25 seasons with the Red Wings in 1970–71, and he's still the franchise's all-time leader in goals (786) and games played (1,687). Howe's 1,023 assists with the Red Wings were a team record until Yzerman came along in 1983; Yzerman retired in 2006 as the Wings' all-time leader in assists with 1,089.

Howe retired with 18 regular-season hat tricks, the most in franchise history. (He also had one in the Stanley Cup Playoffs.) The first came on February 11, 1950, late in his fourth NHL season, when he scored three times in a 9–4 win against the Boston Bruins at Boston Garden. His last hat trick was on November 2, 1969, when Howe scored three times at the Olympia in a 4–3 win against the Pittsburgh Penguins.

Howe's record was largely unchallenged, but 12 years after his departure, Yzerman arrived and began piling up goals.

"Stevie Y" had his first NHL hat trick before his rookie season was three months old. He made it a Merry Christmas for Wings fans by scoring three goals in a 9–2 rout of the Toronto Maple Leafs at Joe Louis Arena on December 23, 1983.

Yzerman had 17 more hat tricks—including a four-goal game against the Edmonton Oilers on January 31, 1990—by the end of the 1992–93 season. And then a strange thing happened.

Though he had yet to turn 28, Yzerman never had another regular-season hat trick, even though he played with the Red Wings through the 2005–06 season. Yzerman did have two more in the Stanley Cup Playoffs, scoring three times against the St. Louis Blues on May 8, 1996, and against the Mighty Ducks of Anaheim on April 21, 1999, giving him four for his career—still a Detroit playoff record—but it is the record of 18 in the regular season that puts him tied with Howe.

40 Even in a high-scoring era, Steve Yzerman was something special. After all, how many players could score goals in nine consecutive games not once, but twice?

Yzerman had already established himself as one of the NHL's top scorers by the 1988–89 season, and he scored 16 goals in his first 17 games before being held without a goal by the Hartford Whalers on November 16, 1988.

He quickly made up for that goal-less game, scoring twice against the Boston Bruins on November 18 and once in the return match two nights later, helping the Red Wings sweep the home-and-home series.

Yzerman had two of Detroit's three goals in an 8–3 loss to the Los Angeles Kings at Joe Louis Arena on November 23, then extended the streak to five games with goals against the Washington Capitals and Winnipeg Jets.

Two goals in a 5–3 home win against the New York Islanders on November 29 ran the streak to six games. He had one goal in each game as the Red Wings split a home-and-home series against the Quebec Nordiques, then scored the first goal of the game at Montreal on December 5, only to have the Canadiens win, 7–2.

The franchise-record nine-game streak ended on December 9, when Yzerman was limited one assist in a 4–3 home win against the Toronto Maple Leafs.

Still, it was a streak for the Red Wings' record book: nine straight games with a goal, 12 goals in all. Who could have guessed he'd duplicate it less than four years later?

Yzerman was actually in a bit of a scoring slump late in January 1992. He'd turned on the red light just twice in the previous nine games when the Buffalo Sabres came to Joe Louis Arena on January 29, but broke out with a hat trick in a 4–4 tie.

Yzerman stayed hot with two goals in each of his next two games, even though the Red Wings lost, 6–3, at home to the New Jersey Devils on January 31 and 4–3 to the Canadiens at Montreal the next night.

A short-handed goal in a 4–4 road tie against the Pittsburgh Penguins extended Yzerman's streak to four games, and he extended it to five by hitting the empty net with two seconds remaining against the Washington Capitals on February 5, wrapping up a 4–1 win.

Yzerman had a goal and an assist in each of Detroit's next three games, with two losses to the Maple Leafs sandwiched around a 5–5 tie against the New York Rangers at Madison Square Garden. He made it nine in a row with two goals in the second period of a 9–4 road win against the Sabres on February 12.

After scoring 14 goals in Detroit's previous nine games, Yzerman's streak came to an end against the San Jose Sharks at Joe Louis Arena on February 15. Though the Red Wings stomped the first-year Sharks, 11–1, Yzerman was limited to two assists.

OK. You've had some time to get a little rest, maybe grab some refreshment and listen to a few words about what you can do better in the next 20 minutes. It's time to lace 'em up again and get ready for Period No. 2. Here we go . . .

1 The Red Wings were part of the NHL's expansion from seven to 10 teams in 1926, They entered the league along with two other teams. Which teams came into the NHL with the Wings, known then as the Detroit Cougars? *Answer on page 77.*
  a. Chicago Black Hawks and Boston Bruins
  b. Chicago Black Hawks and New York Rangers
  c. Montreal Maroons and New York Rangers
  d. New York Rangers and Ottawa Senators

2 Defenseman Chris Chelios was once quoted as saying he would never play for the Red Wings. That changed in 1999, when he was traded to Detroit and spent the next decade on the blue line at Joe Louis Arena. From which team did the Red Wings acquire Chelios, and what was the price? *Answers on page 78.*

3 Few players won as much hardware as Gordie Howe. How many times did Mr. Hockey win the Hart Trophy as the NHL's most valuable player? *Answer on page 80.*
  a. 3
  b. 4
  c. 5
  d. 6

4 The Red Wings famously won the Stanley Cup in 1950 by rallying to defeat the New York Rangers in seven games. They had to do it without one of their biggest stars, who was out with an injury. Which Detroit legend spent the playoffs on the sidelines? Give yourself an extra point if you know what the injury was. *Answers on page 81.*
   a. Sid Abel
   b. Gordie Howe
   c. Ted Lindsay
   d. Terry Sawchuk

5 One of the great rivalries in the NHL during the late 1990s and early 2000s involved the Red Wings. Which team was their biggest nemesis during that time? *Answer on page 83.*
   a. Chicago Blackhawks
   b. Colorado Avalanche
   c. Edmonton Oilers
   d. Toronto Maple Leafs

6 Hockey Hall of Famer Red Kelly owns eight Stanley Cup rings, the most of any NHL player who never suited up for the Montreal Canadiens. How many of those rings did he win with the Red Wings? *Answer on page 85.*
   a. 4
   b. 5
   c. 6
   d. 7

7 One price the Red Wings paid for their success in the 1990s, 2000s, and 2010s is that they went more than 25 years without a top-10 pick in the NHL draft. That ended in 2017, when Detroit took forward Michael Rasmussen with the No. 9 pick. Before Rasmussen, who was the last player taken by

the Red Wings with a pick among the first 10 in the draft? *Answer on page 88.*
a. Johan Franzen
b. Martin Lapointe
c. Dylan Larkin
d. Keith Primeau

8 The Red Wings had a legendary talent haul in the 1989 NHL Draft, including two players taken after the first round who are now enshrined in the Hockey Hall of Fame. How many players taken by the Wings in that draft played at least 1,000 NHL regular-season games? *Answer on page 89.*
a. 2
b. 3
c. 4
d. 5

9 After being swept by the New Jersey Devils in the 1995 Stanley Cup Final, the Red Wings decided they needed more grit among their bottom-six forwards in order to counteract units such as New Jersey's "Crash Line." What was the name of the trio assembled by coach Scotty Bowman, and who were the members? *Answers on page 91.*

10 The Red Wings have had a number of Hall of Fame players who've wound up behind the bench. Which of these Red Wings stars did *not* end up coaching them? *Answer on page 93.*
a. Alex Delvecchio
b. Bill Gadsby
c. Gordie Howe
d. Ted Lindsay

11 Match the player to his nickname. *Answer on page 94.*

Alex Delvecchio   The Perfect Human
Pavel Datsyuk   The Professor
Johan Franzen   Fats
Nicklas Lidstrom   Magic Man
Igor Larionov   Mule

12 The Red Wings were involved in the longest game in NHL history. They needed six overtimes to defeat the Montreal Maroons, 1–0, in Game 1 of the 1936 Semifinals. Who scored the goal that won the game, and who was the winning goaltender? You get a bonus point if you know how many saves he made. *Answers on page 97.*

13 Five Red Wings have won the Conn Smythe Trophy as the most valuable player of the Stanley Cup Playoffs, but only one has done it while playing for the losing team. Who was it? *Answer on page 98.*
   a. Roger Crozier
   b. Gordie Howe
   c. Nicklas Lidstrom
   d. Terry Sawchuk

14 The Red Wings have had 11 seasons in which a player scored 50 or more goals. Steve Yzerman owns five of them. Who is the only other player with more than one? *Answer on page 100.*
   a. Sergei Fedorov
   b. Gordie Howe
   c. Mickey Redmond
   d. John Ogrodnick

15 Just two Red Wings have had 70 or more assists in a single season. Steve Yzerman did it twice, with 90 in 1988–89 and 79 in 1992–93. Who is the only other Detroit player to have a 70-assist season? *Answer on page 101.*

a. Alex Delvecchio
b. Marcel Dionne
c. Sergei Fedorov
d. Nicklas Lidstrom

16 The Red Wings won the Stanley Cup three times under Scotty Bowman after hiring him as coach in 1993. Who did Bowman replace behind the bench? *Answer on page 103.*
a. Mike Babcock
b. Jacques Demers
c. Mike Keenan
d. Bryan Murray

17 Mike Vernon was the goaltender for the Red Wings when they won the Stanley Cup in 1997. From which team did the Wings acquire Vernon? There's an extra point if you know when they brought him to Detroit. *Answers on page 104.*
a. Calgary Flames
b. Edmonton Oilers
c. Florida Panthers
d. San Jose Sharks

18 The Ted Lindsay Award, formerly the Lester B. Pearson Award, is named after one of the Red Wings' icons and given to the outstanding player of the regular season as voted by members of the NHL Players' Association. How many Red Wings have won the award, and who are they? *Answers on page 105.*

19 The 1999–2000 season was full of milestones for Red Wings legend Steve Yzerman. Which of these was *not* one of them? *Answer on page 106.*
a. 900th career assist
b. 100th game-winning goal
c. 600th goal
d. 1,500th point

20 Nicklas Lidstrom is one of the greatest defensemen in NHL history, as evidenced by the fact that he won the Norris Trophy seven times. Who is the only player to have won the Norris Trophy more times than Lidstrom? *Answer on page 107.*
   a. Paul Coffey
   b. Doug Harvey
   c. Bobby Orr
   d. Pierre Pilote

21 The Lady Byng Trophy is presented to the player who combines on-ice skill with gentlemanly play. Only three defensemen have won the award since it was established in 1924. Two of them played for the Red Wings. Who are they? *Answer on page 109.*

22 Gordie Howe led the Red Wings in scoring for 13 of 15 seasons from 1955–56 through 1969–70. Who was Detroit's leading scorer in the other two seasons of that time span? *Answer on page 110.*
   a. Alex Delvecchio
   b. Marcel Dionne
   c. Ted Lindsay
   d. Norm Ullman

23 Three goalies in Red Wings history have won 40 or more games in a season. Who is the only one to do it more than once? *Answer on page 111.*
   a. Roger Crozier
   b. Dominik Hasek
   c. Chris Osgood
   d. Terry Sawchuk

24 The days of one goalie playing all of his team's games are long gone. Who is the last goaltender in Wings history to play in every minute of all of Detroit's games in one season, and when did it happen? *Answers on page 112.*

25 The Red Wings have scored in double figures 32 times in their history. When did the most recent one take place? *Answer on page 114.*
a. 1994
b. 1995
c. 1997
d. 2002

26 A hat trick by a defenseman is an NHL rarity. Who was the last Detroit defenseman to get one? *Answer on page 115.*
a. Mike Green
b. Reed Larson
c. Nicklas Lidstrom
d. Mathieu Schneider

27 It took the Red Wings until 1933 to win a game in the Stanley Cup Playoffs. They didn't win one in either 1929 or 1932, their first two appearances in the postseason. Which team did the Red Wings defeat to earn their first playoff victory? *Answer on page 116.*
a. Boston Bruins
b. Montreal Canadiens
c. Montreal Maroons
d. New York Rangers

28 Four players in NHL history have played 1,500 or more games and spent their entire career with the same team. Three of the four are Red Wings. (The fourth is Shane Doan, who did it with the Winnipeg Jets/Arizona Coyotes.) Who are the three lifers who spent their whole careers with the Wings? *Answer on page 117.*

29 In 1987 and 1988, the Red Wings were within one round of advancing to the Stanley Cup Final before being eliminated. They lost to the same team each time. Which team twice spoiled Detroit's hopes of getting to the Final? *Answer on page 118.*
   a. Chicago Blackhawks
   b. Edmonton Oilers
   c. Los Angeles Kings
   d. Toronto Maple Leafs

30 Hall of Fame defenseman Nicklas Lidstrom was one of the keys to the Red Wings' run of success from the early 1990s into the 2010s. He finished his career with a plus-450 rating, meaning he was on the ice for 450 more non-power play goals by the Wings than by the opposition. How many times in his 20 NHL seasons was Lidstrom a minus player? *Answer on page 119.*
   a. 0
   b. 1
   c. 3
   d. 5

31 Steve Yzerman scored one of the most famous goals in franchise history to give the Red Wings a 1–0 double-overtime win in Game 7 of the 1996 Western Conference Semifinals. Which team did the Red Wings outlast in the series? *Answer on page 120.*
   a. Chicago Blackhawks
   b. Los Angeles Kings
   c. Phoenix Coyotes
   d. St. Louis Blues

32 The Red Wings had a Hall of Famer as their No. 1 goaltender in every season from 1944–45 through 1963–64. Terry Sawchuk was between the pipes for 12 of those seasons. Which goaltender preceded him, and who took his place for two seasons in the 1950s? *Answers on page 121.*

33 The Red Wings called the Olympia (also known as Olympia Stadium) home from 1927 to 1979. Who were the opponents on opening and closing night? *Answer on page 123.*

34 Detroit is the only team in NHL history to win a championship by scoring an overtime goal in Game 7 of the Stanley Cup Final. How many times have the Red Wings won the ultimate prize in hockey by scoring in OT? *Answer on page 126.*
   a. 1
   b. 2
   c. 3
   d. 4

35 Gordie Howe was a regular fixture in the NHL All-Star Game during his 2 1/2 decades with the Red Wings. How many times was Mr. Hockey selected to play in the game during his time with Detroit? *Answer on page 127.*
   a. 19
   b. 20
   c. 21
   d. 22

36 Steve Yzerman is the last Red Wing to wear No. 19. It was raised to the rafters of Joe Louis Arena on January 2, 2007, a few months after he retired. Yzerman wore No. 19 in honor of a player he admired and wound up competing against. Who is the Hockey Hall of Famer Yzerman admired so much that he asked to wear his number? *Answer on page 128.*

37 One of the sweetest wins in Red Wings history came in Game 7 of the 2002 Western Conference Final. The victory put Detroit into the Stanley Cup Final, but what made it especially enjoyable for the Wings and their fans? *Answer on page 128.*

38 The Red Wings won at least 43 games in eight of nine full seasons during Mike Babcock's decade as coach from 2005 to 2015. But just as Superman had his Kryptonite, there was one unlikely team that dominated the Red Wings during Babcock's tenure. Which team, one that struggled for most of Babcock's time in Detroit, got the better of the Wings during that decade? *Answer on page 130.*
  a. Anaheim Ducks
  b. Dallas Stars
  c. New York Islanders
  d. Washington Capitals

39 Tossing an octopus is a Detroit playoff tradition. In what year did the first octopus hit the ice at the Olympia? *Answer on page 131.*
  a. 1950
  b. 1952
  c. 1954
  d. 1955

40 The Red Wings traded away goaltender Terry Sawchuk after winning the 1955 Stanley Cup, but decided two years later they wanted him back. Which future Hall of Famer did they send to the Boston Bruins to bring Sawchuk back to Detroit? *Answer on page 132.*
  a. Johnny Bucyk
  b. Fern Flaman
  c. Glenn Hall
  d. Milt Schmidt

There's the horn. The second period is in the books. Time to tromp back to the locker room, get some hydration, listen to a few well-chosen words from the coaching staff and prepare to come out ready for the third period.

SECOND PERIOD—
ANSWERS

1 The National Hockey League was a seven-team, one-division league in 1925–26, with the Ottawa Senators winning the regular-season championship but losing to the Montreal Maroons in the league final. The Maroons went on to defeat the Victoria Cougars of the Western Hockey League to win the Stanley Cup. It was the last time a non-NHL team played for the Cup, as the WHL folded after the season.

Three of the seven teams played in the United States—the Boston Bruins had joined the NHL in 1924, followed by the New York Americans and Pittsburgh Pirates a year later—and now the NHL was looking to expand its footprint in the US.

When league officials met on April 18, 1926, they faced a host of applications. Madison Square Garden, where the Americans rented ice for their home games, wanted a team of its own. Groups from Detroit, Chicago, Cleveland, New Jersey, and Hamilton, Ontario, also were interested in bringing an NHL team to their cities.

The application by Madison Square Garden to ice a team, which became the New York Rangers, was approved quickly. But the NHL decided to do additional due diligence on the other hopefuls. There was opposition among some teams to adding more than one team, while at the time the league constitution said any expansion had to be approved by unanimous vote.

The Americans, in particular, weren't in favor of a team in Detroit. They preferred to have two teams in Chicago, as eventually would be the case in New York. But on May 2, 1926, the league amended its constitution to make expansion possible by a mere majority vote. After that, it seemed predestined that Chicago and Detroit would join the Rangers as new NHL teams for the 1926–27 season.

On May 15, 1926, a group of investors was tentatively awarded a Detroit franchise, on condition that there would be an arena ready for the 1926–27 season. With the WHL in its death throes, Lester and Frank Patrick sold the Victoria Cougars to the Detroit group for $100,000. The owners kept the nickname "Cougars." Perhaps oddly, the NHL doesn't consider the current Red Wings to be a continuation of the Victoria franchise.

However, the arena, which later became known as Olympia Stadium (or merely "The Olympia"), wasn't ready, forcing the new team to play its first season in Windsor, Ontario. But the franchise was permanently approved on September 25, 1926, the same day as the new Chicago franchise, known as the Black Hawks. (The team changed to the one word "Blackhawks" in 1986.) All three newcomers made their NHL debuts for the 1926–27 season.

2 Chris Chelios began his NHL career with the Montreal Canadiens after playing for the United States at the 1984 Sarajevo Olympics. He was traded to the Chicago Blackhawks in the summer of 1990 and soon seemed like an institution in his hometown. Chelios was one of the NHL's best defensemen even as he seemed headed toward the end of his career in 1998–99. Indeed, the 37-year-old, a three-time Norris Trophy winner, looked like he might play out the remainder of his NHL career in the city where he'd been born.

Chelios was one of those players opposing fans loved to boo—and Detroit fans were no exception. The idea that he could end up with the Red Wings seemed preposterous.

But the Blackhawks had hit the skids in the late 1990s, missing the playoffs in 1998 and on track to do the same thing in 1999. As the NHL trade deadline approached, the Hawks began to consider moving out some of their older players. Meanwhile, the Red Wings were trying for a three-peat and felt they needed some help on defense.

Chelios had voiced his dislike of the Red Wings on multiple occasions, stating they were overrated and vowing he'd never, ever go to Detroit. To top it off, he had a no-trade clause to back him up.

Hall of Fame defenseman Chris Chelios won the Stanley Cup with the Red Wings in 2002 and 2008 after being acquired from the Chicago Blackhawks. (dan4th - 080202 red wings at bruins (120); License: CC BY 2.0 Source: https: //commons.wikimedia.org/w/index.php?curid=4833545)

But whether it was the possibility of winning the Stanley Cup for the second time (he'd played on Montreal's championship team in 1986), or some other reason known only to him, Chelios opted to waive his no-trade clause when the Red Wings inquired about acquiring him.

On March 23, 1999, the Red Wings got their man. Chelios was traded to the Red Wings for defenseman Anders Eriksson and Detroit's first-round picks in the 1999 and 2001 NHL drafts.

That might have seemed like a big price for a 37-year-old defenseman. In truth, it turned out to be a bargain. Eriksson, who had been Detroit's first-round pick (No. 22) in the 1993 NHL Draft, played in the NHL for most of the next decade but never became an impact player. Neither did forward Steve McCarthy and goaltender Adam Munro, the players the Blackhawks selected with the two first-round picks.

In contrast, Chelios proved to be a lot more than a rental. He spent the next decade with the Red Wings, helping Detroit win the Cup in 2002 and 2008. He was named a First-Team All-Star in 2002, at age 40, and ended up playing 578 games with the Wings.

3 With the exception of Wayne Gretzky, who won it nine times, no player has won the Hart Trophy, given by the NHL to "the player adjudged the most valuable to his team," more than Gordie Howe.

But unlike Gretzky, who won the Hart in each of his first eight NHL seasons, missed in one season, and then won his ninth MVP award, Howe spread his over a span of 12 seasons.

Howe led the NHL in scoring in 1950–51, his fifth NHL season, but ended up in a tie for third with teammate Red Kelly in balloting for the Hart, with Milt Schmidt of the Boston Bruins finishing first and Maurice Richard of the Montreal Canadiens coming in second. In 1951–52, Howe again led the NHL in scoring, again finishing with 86 points in 70 games, and this time was recognized as the league's MVP. He received nine of the 16 first-place votes and finished well ahead of Montreal center Elmer Lach.

Howe was even better in 1952–53, again leading the NHL in scoring and setting a league record with 95 points, including 49 goals. The Red Wings finished first in the regular-season standings, and Howe cruised to another MVP award, finishing first on nine of the 16 ballots. His 58 points were more than the combined totals of Kelly and Chicago Black Hawks goaltender Al Rollins, who tied for second.

Despite leading the NHL in scoring again in 1953–54, Howe came in fourth in the Hart Trophy race. In 1954–55, he had 62 points in 64 games and didn't even get a vote for the Hart—the last time that happened until 1970–71, his final season with the Red Wings.

Howe had 79 points, including 38 goals, in 1955–56 and finished seventh in the Hart Trophy balloting. But he took home the Hart for the third time in 1956–57 after leading the NHL in scoring with 89 points, including a league-high 44 goals.

Though Howe didn't lead the NHL in scoring in 1957–58, he finished with 77 points in 64 games, enough to win the Hart for the fourth time. He finished comfortably ahead of New York Rangers right wing Andy Bathgate.

The voting was flipped in 1958–59, with Bathgate finishing ahead of Howe despite the fact the Rangers collapsed down the stretch and finished out of the Stanley Cup Playoffs. However, Howe made it five MVP awards in 1959–60, even though his scoring totals were comparatively low for him: "just" 28 goals and 73 points.

Howe averaged more than a point a game in 1960–61 and 1961–62 and drew a good measure of support in the Hart balloting each season, but came in third and fourth, respectively.

His sixth and final Hart Trophy came in 1962–63, when he led the NHL in goals (38) and points (86), finishing well ahead of Chicago Black Hawks center Stan Mikita.

Though Howe was a First-Team or Second-Team All-Star in each of the next seven seasons, he never finished better than third in the voting for the Hart Trophy. Not until 1970–71 was he completely omitted from the voting.

Aside from Gretzky and Howe, no player has won the Hart Trophy more than four times. The 12 years between his first and last MVP awards represent the longest gap in NHL history.

4 The 1949–50 Red Wings were a powerhouse. They lapped the field during the regular season, winning the Prince of Wales Trophy as the NHL's top finisher with a record of 37–19–14. Their 88 points were 11 more than the second-place Montreal Canadiens.

The Red Wings led the NHL in goals scored with 229. The last-place Chicago Black Hawks were next at 203. The Wings' 164 goals allowed were the second-fewest behind the 150 surrendered by Montreal.

Detroit's famed "Production Line" dominated the scoring race. Left wing Ted Lindsay won the Art Ross Trophy as the NHL's leading scorer with 78 points, followed by center Sid Abel with 69 and Gordie Howe with 68. Goalie Harry Lumley was tops in the NHL with 33 wins and second to Montreal's Bill Durnan with a 2.35 goals-against average.

The Wings were a huge favorite to capture the Stanley Cup when they opened their Semifinal series against the third-place Toronto Maple Leafs, the three-time defending NHL champions, at the Olympia, on March 28. But they suffered a huge loss in that game when Howe went down with a head injury that ended his season—and nearly his life.

The Leafs jumped out to a 3–0 lead in Game 1. In the second period, Howe, three days shy of his 22nd birthday, came charging towards Ted "Teeder" Kennedy as the Toronto captain spearheaded a rush through center ice. But Kennedy saw out of the corner of his eye that he was about to be hammered into the boards, so he abruptly pulled up.

Howe stumbled, glanced off his intended target, and went head-first into the top of the boards in front of the Detroit bench. Teammate "Black Jack" Stewart couldn't stop his momentum and fell over Howe.

The result was catastrophic. Stewart got up but Howe stayed on the ice, unmoving. He was bleeding and unconscious. As the packed house watched in stunned silence, Howe was stretchered off the ice, taken into the dressing room for assessment and then rushed by ambulance to Harper Hospital.

Howe had broken his nose, shattered his cheekbone, and seriously scratched his right eye. More important, it seemed probable he'd fractured his skull.

His brain hemorrhaged. Shortly after midnight, a neurosurgeon began a delicate, life-saving operation. An opening was drilled into Howe's skull, from which the surgeon drained fluid to relieve pressure on the brain. After the 90-minute operation, Howe was put in an oxygen tent.

Happily, the operation was a success, and Howe wound up pulling through. Fourth-graders at a local Catholic school felt they'd had a hand in his recovery. Their teacher was Lindsay's sister, and she had asked them to pray for a special friend of hers.

Although Kennedy was widely vilified, an inquiry by the NHL cleared him of any blame in the accident. Kennedy always maintained that the only thing he was guilty of was getting out of the way. Though many of the Wings agreed with that view in private, the team's public stance was outrage; the organization contended that Kennedy had butt-ended Howe in the eye, causing him to crash into the boards.

The Red Wings lost, 5–0, in Game 1 and trailed the series, 3–2, before Lumley blanked the Leafs in Game 6. Lumley and Toronto's Turk Broda matched saves through three periods in Game 7 before Leo Reise, whose goal 38 seconds into double overtime had won Game 4, scored 8:39 into OT for a 1–0 victory that eliminated the Leafs and sent the Wings into the Final against the New York Rangers.

The Howe-less Red Wings got all they could handle from the Rangers before winning Game 7 in double overtime for their first of four championships in a span of six seasons.

5 By the mid-1990s, the Red Wings had established themselves as one of the NHL's elite teams. They'd won their division in 1993–94 (though they were upset by the San Jose Sharks in the first round of the Stanley Cup Playoffs), got to the Final in 1995 (but were swept by the New Jersey Devils), and set an NHL regular-season record for wins in 1995–96, before being eliminated by the Colorado Avalanche in six games in the Western Conference Final.

Game 6 of that series lit the fuse on one of the most intense rivalries during the next few seasons.

Just over 14 minutes into the game, Colorado's Claude Lemieux checked Detroit center Kris Draper from behind, sending him face-first into the boards. The hit sent Draper to the hospital with a broken jaw, as well as shattered cheek and orbital bones. He required reconstructive surgery that necessitated having his jaw wired shut, and there were numerous stitches.

Lemieux received a major penalty for checking from behind and a game misconduct. Detroit's Paul Coffey scored during the ensuing five-minute power play to tie the game, 1–1, but Colorado scored three times in the second period for a series-clinching 4–1 victory and went on to sweep the Florida Panthers to win the Stanley Cup in their first season in Denver after the franchise moved from Quebec.

The teams held the traditional handshake after the Avalanche eliminated the Red Wings, although forward Dino Ciccarelli said of his encounter with Lemieux, "I can't believe I shook this guy's friggin' hand after the game. That pisses me right off."

The teams played three times during the 1996–97 season without a major incident. Colorado won all three games, giving the Avs seven wins in nine tries against the Wings. But the fourth game, on March 26, 1997, at Joe Louis Arena, was the Red Wings' night for revenge.

Two defensemen, Colorado's Brent Severyn and Detroit's Jamie Pushor, fought 4:46 into the game. Next, forwards Kirk Maltby of the Wings and Rene Corbet of the Avs squared off at 10:14. But with Colorado leading, 1–0, late in the first period, the real fireworks broke out at 18:22.

After a collision between Detroit center Igor Larionov and Colorado's Peter Forsberg, Detroit's Darren McCarty took the opportunity to avenge Lemieux's attack on Draper. He escaped the linesman who was trying to control him and blindsided Lemieux with a right hook. Lemieux turtled as McCarty rained punches on him, and then McCarty dragged Lemieux to the boards and kneed him in the head before officials were able to get him away.

Avs goaltender Patrick Roy wanted to get in on the action, but he was clotheslined by Detroit's Brendan Shanahan. After Detroit goalie Mike Vernon tried to pull Colorado defenseman Adam Foote off Shanahan, Roy pulled him away, the two goaltenders dropped their masks and gloves, then staged one of the more memorable goalie fights in NHL history.

The outcome left the Wings down a man; McCarty's double minor for roughing was the only unmatched penalty. Just 15 seconds later, Detroit's Vladimir Konstantinov and Colorado forward Adam Deadmarsh went at it.

There were five more fights in the second period, which ended with Colorado ahead, 4–3. Valeri Kamensky's goal early in the third period put Colorado ahead, 5–3, but the Red Wings tied it on goals by Martin Lapointe and Shanahan, then won it when McCarty scored 39 seconds into overtime.

The teams went at it again on May 22, during Game 4 of the Western Conference Final. Though the outcome was long settled (the Wings won, 6–0), the teams had four fights in the third period. Colorado coach Marc Crawford screamed obscenities at his Detroit counterpart, Scotty Bowman, across the glass between the benches. The tirade earned him a $10,000 fine from the NHL.

The Red Wings went on to eliminate the Avs and win the Cup, but the fireworks weren't over.

On November 11, 1997, McCarty and Lemieux began exchanging punches three seconds after the opening faceoff at Joe Louis Arena, delighting the sellout crowd that saw Lemieux as Public Enemy No. 1.

The Avs came back to Detroit for a game on April 1, 1998, that featured 228 penalty minutes and another battle between the goaltenders. With 7:11 remaining, Roy challenged Detroit's Chris Osgood. The two fought at center ice, earning fighting penalties and game misconducts and forcing each team to use its backup goaltender to finish the game, a 2–0 win for the Avalanche.

Roster turnover on both sides began to water down the rivalry. The last big scrap between the teams took place in the third period at Pepsi Center in Denver on March 23, 2002. Shortly after the Wings had taken a 1–0 lead, Maltby crashed the net and Roy took exception. Detroit goaltender Dominik Hasek skated the length of the ice, and only the intervention of the officials kept Roy from fighting his third different Detroit goaltender in five years.

The Red Wings got the ultimate revenge in Game 7 of the 2002 Western Conference Final. With the packed house at Joe Louis Arena bellowing its approval, the Wings stomped the Avs, 7–0. Six of the goals came against Roy, who was lifted after two periods. The Red Wings went on to their third championship in six seasons.

6 Red Kelly had a career almost unparalleled in hockey. He was an elite defenseman for more than a decade with the Red Wings, then went on to a second life as one of the NHL's best two-way centers with the Toronto Maple Leafs.

Kelly is often forgotten today, a relic from an era in which few

NHL games were on television and the league was a collection of six teams that went no further west than Chicago. He didn't have the kind of flashy style that drew a lot of attention; rather, he was the kind of player you had to watch night in and night out to really appreciate.

The guys he played with and against had no such problem recognizing his abilities.

"Red was the best," Gordie Howe said when he was interviewed by Rich Kincaide for his book *The Gods of Olympia Stadium*. "He was very much a mobile defenseman like Doug Harvey. Red was a better skater. And he was strong."

It's hard to believe now, but Kelly's skating originally kept him from making the junior clubs at St. Michael's in Toronto. But his hockey IQ was so apparent that the coaching staff reconsidered, and his work ethic helped him improve his game. With some help from one of his heroes, former Maple Leafs star Joe Primeau, he became a star in junior hockey and attracted the attention of the Red Wings. After St. Michael's won the Memorial Cup in 1947, Kelly went straight to Detroit, never spending a day in the minor leagues.

Among the lessons Kelly learned from Primeau was to control his temper—after all, no one has ever scored a goal from the penalty box. Kelly played hard but clean. In nearly 13 full seasons with the Red Wings, he never had more than 39 penalty minutes in a season and won the Lady Byng Trophy for skillful and gentlemanly play three times, the last in 1953–54. No defenseman won the award again until Brian Campbell of the Florida Panthers did it in 2011–12.

Kelly did more than keep the puck out of Detroit's net. In an era when defenseman weren't big offensive contributors, he had at least 15 goals and 40 points per season from 1949–50 through 1955–56. He won the Norris Trophy as the NHL's top defenseman in 1954 and was a First-Team or Second-Team NHL All-Star from 1949–50 through 1956–57.

Kelly was so exceptional defensively that his coaches took advantage of his superb conditioning by giving him all the ice time he could handle. He recalled in *Legends of Hockey* that coach Tommy Ivan "used me as much as 55 minutes in a game in Detroit. I was always in great

Red Kelly played on four Stanley Cup-winning teams with the Red Wings as a defenseman and four more with the Toronto Maple Leafs as a center. (Associated Press)

shape; I guess that helped keep me in great shape, and whenever you want me to go, I went."

Kelly was a key to one of hockey's great teams. The Red Wings finished first for an NHL-record eight straight seasons and won the Stanley Cup in 1950, 1952, 1954, and 1955.

In the end, Kelly's eagerness to help the team turned out to be the reason for his departure from Detroit. When management asked him to play shortly after he broke an ankle in the latter stages of the 1958–59 season, Kelly had the ankle taped and returned to the lineup, missing only a handful of games. But his play was below his usual standard, and Detroit missed the playoffs for the first time in 21 seasons. Because news of the injury had been kept secret, there were rumors that Kelly was washed up, but after he healed and rebounded the following autumn, he told a reporter about the injury. General manager Jack Adams was furious and traded Kelly to the New York Rangers.

Kelly refused to go, insisting he'd had enough and was going to retire. The trade was nullified, and Kelly quickly got a job with a tool company in Detroit. But just a few days later, Maple Leafs coach and GM Punch Imlach was able to talk him out of retirement. The Leafs and Wings worked out a deal for Kelly's rights—at 32 years old, Kelly was living his childhood dream of skating for the Maple Leafs.

Imlach converted Kelly into a center with the idea that he'd be perfect for shutting down stars like Montreal's Jean Beliveau. The strategy worked so well that the Maple Leafs won four Cups in six seasons—1962, 1963, 1964, and 1967. Kelly retired after the fourth Cup, his eighth . . . and Toronto hasn't won one since.

7 There's a price for everything. For the Red Wings, the price they paid for making the Stanley Cup Playoffs for 25 consecutive seasons was not picking high in the NHL draft. Unlike the 1980s, when the Red Wings usually picked very high—Steve Yzerman was the fourth player taken in 1983—beginning in 1992, they had no pick in the top 10 until 2017.

Before they took Michael Rasmussen with the No. 9 choice in '17, the last player taken by the Wings with a top-10 pick was Martin Lapointe, who was selected as No. 10 in 1991.

Lapointe, a center, was coming off seasons of 42 and 44 goals with the Laval Titans of the Quebec Major Junior Hockey League when he was taken by the Red Wings in 1991. By the end of the 1991–92 season, he was already playing in the NHL.

Lapointe played four regular-season games and three Stanley Cup Playoff games. He scored 25 goals in 28 games with the Adirondack Red Wings of the American Hockey League in 1993–94 and had eight goals and 16 points in 50 games with Detroit. After spending the first part of the 1994–95 season with Adirondack while the NHL was idled because of the owners' lockout, Lapointe joined the Red Wings after play resumed and never looked back.

Though Lapointe had been a big scorer in junior hockey, his role in the NHL was more of a checking center—and, to be fair, on a team that had Steve Yzerman and Sergei Fedorov, there aren't many players who'd have been a first- or second-line center ahead of those two.

But Lapointe had his uses. He had 63 goals and 137 points in a span of four seasons from 1996–97 through 1999–2000 and played on Detroit's Stanley Cup-winning teams in 1997 and 1998.

Lapointe had a breakout season offensively in 2000–01, scoring 27 goals and finishing with 57 points. His timing was perfect. The big numbers came just before he was due to become a free agent and earned him a four-year, $20 million contract with the Boston Bruins. Unfortunately for his new employers, Lapointe reverted to form as a checking center who was a useful, but not prolific offensive contributor. He never had more than 15 goals or 40 points in a season again before retiring in 2008.

8 The 1989 NHL Draft marked a turning point for the Red Wings. Few teams have helped themselves more in the span of a few hours than the Wings did on June 17, 1989, at Met Center in Bloomington, Minnesota. After all, how many teams select four 1,000-game players on the same day?

"I don't think there was a better draft in the history of hockey than our draft, the Red Wings' draft, in '89," general manager Jim Devellano told NHL.com in 2015. "I'm also here to tell you there was some luck involved."

Truer words were never spoken. The Red Wings selected two future Hockey Hall of Famers in 1989, although neither went in the first round. Instead, the Wings chose center Mike Sillinger from the Regina Pats of the Western Hockey League with the 11th pick in the opening round.

Sillinger was coming off a 53-goal, 131-point season with Regina when the Red Wings selected him. He returned to the Pats for two seasons, scoring 57 and 50 goals in his age-19 and -20 seasons. But he never came close to those numbers in an NHL career that saw him play with a league-record 12 teams.

His best offensive season came as a 35 year old, when he scored 26 goals and finished with 59 points for the New York Islanders in 2006–07. He retired from the NHL two years later with 240 goals and 548 points in 1,049 games, though just 128 with the Wings.

Rugged defenseman Bob Boughner went to the Wings in the second round. He ended up playing 630 NHL games with six teams, none of them with the Red Wings, who traded him to the Buffalo Sabres while he was still in the minor leagues.

The idea that Boughner was picked ahead of Nicklas Lidstrom seems almost laughable now; Lidstrom went on to become one of the top half-dozen defensemen in NHL history and was inducted into the Hockey Hall of Fame in 2015, his first year of eligibility.

But scouting in 1989 wasn't nearly as thorough as it is today. The Red Wings were one of the few teams that had scouted Lidstrom extensively and did their best to keep word of their interest in him from leaking out. They were able to nab him in the third round (No. 53). Lidstrom stayed in Sweden for two more seasons before coming to the Wings in 1991. He never left, finishing his Hall of Fame career with 264 goals and 1,142 points in 1,564 games, all with the Wings.

Finding a player like Lidstrom in any round of a draft would be enough for most teams. But Detroit made it back-to-back future Hall of Famers when Russian center Sergei Fedorov was taken in the fourth round (No. 74).

Fedorov wasn't exactly a secret. He had centered a line with Alexander Mogilny and Pavel Bure that had helped the Soviet Union win the World Junior Championship and was regarded as one of the best young talents in hockey. He lasted as long as he did because there was no certainty he'd ever be able to play in North America.

Earlier in 1989, Mogilny had become the first defector from the USSR to play in the NHL when he joined the Buffalo Sabres. Jim Lites, then an executive vice president and chief operating officer of the Red Wings, met with Fedorov a few months later and offered to help him defect. But Fedorov said he wanted to finish his season with the Soviet Red Army team and complete his military service so as not to be branded a traitor before making any move.

The Goodwill Games, a creation of media mogul Ted Turner, were held in the USSR in 1986 and were scheduled for 1990 in Seattle. Though the Games were to be held in the summer, there was to be a hockey competition. After an exhibition game in Portland, Oregon, Fedorov defected and was flown to Detroit. He spent his first 13 NHL seasons with the Red Wings and played in three Stanley Cup champions in Detroit. Fedorov played 1,248 games, finishing with 483 goals and 1,179 points before returning to Russia for three more seasons.

But Devellano wasn't finished with this draft. In the sixth round, the Wings took center Dallas Drake, who ended up playing 1,009 games and scoring 177 goals. He spent his first two seasons with Detroit, then returned to the Wings in 2007–08 and retired after the Wings won the Stanley Cup.

But for a tragic accident, there could have been five 1,000-game players in the 1989 draft. Defenseman Vladimir Konstantinov, Detroit's 11th-round pick (No. 221), played in 446 games in a career that was cut short by a limo accident he was involved in the day after the Red Wings won the Stanley Cup in 1997.

"It can't happen again, because guys like Lidstrom and Fedorov, now they go in the top five," Ken Holland, who went on to become Detroit's GM, told NHL.com. "It's a different time. You can't have those kinds of drafts. You can still get three, four, or five players out of a draft, but you're not going to get two Hall of Famers and a bunch of people who will play in 1,000 games."

9 The Red Wings were favored to defeat the New Jersey Devils when the teams faced off in the 1995 Stanley Cup Final. The Devils had finished fifth in the Eastern Conference during the lockout-shortened 1994–95 season with a 22–18–8 record, while the Red Wings won the Presidents' Trophy by going 33–11–4.

But the Devils caught fire during the Stanley Cup Playoffs, capping the franchise's first championship by sweeping the Red Wings in the Final. One reason for the Devils' success was their "Crash Line" of Bobby Holik between Mike Peluso and Randy McKay. All three were 200-plus pounds and played a physical brand of hockey that made life miserable for opponents. They could also put the puck in the net, but their main function was to crash and bang.

It's said that imitation is the sincerest form of flattery, and the Wings decided they needed their own version of the "Crash Line." Coach Scotty Bowman found what he was looking for when he put center Kris Draper together with wingers Kirk Maltby and Joe Kocur. Draper provided speed and the ability to win faceoffs, Maltby was an excellent checker, and Kocur was one of the NHL's true heavyweights.

When the Red Wings made it back to the Final, in 1997, against the Philadelphia Flyers, the "Grind Line" spurred the Wings to a sweep for their first Cup since 1955. The trio stayed together to help the Wings win again in 1998.

Darren McCarty took Kocur's spot on the line after the 1997–98 season (Kocur retired in 1999), and the trio stayed together through

Darren McCarty was part of the "Grind Line" that did a lot of the dirty work on Detroit's Cup-winning teams. (Associated Press)

the 2003–04 season. When play resumed after the 2004–05 lockout, the Red Wings bought out McCarty, who spent the next two seasons with the Calgary Flames before returning to the Wings in 2007–08 and reuniting with his old linemates in time to help Detroit win the Cup again.

10 For decades, NHL teams liked to stay in-house when selecting a new coach or general manager. The Red Wings were no different. Several of their biggest stars spent time behind the bench or in the front office after their playing days were done.

Ted Lindsay was a star with the Wings in the 1940s and 1950s. After retiring, he became a broadcaster for several years before rejoining the Red Wings in 1977 as their general manager. The Red Wings returned to the Stanley Cup Playoffs in 1978, and Lindsay was voted the NHL's executive of the year. He named himself coach late in the 1979–80 season but was fired after Detroit went 3–14–3 to start the 1980–81 season.

Bill Gadsby was a defenseman who spent the last five seasons (1961 to 1966) of his Hall of Fame career with the Red Wings. Two seasons after leaving the Red Wings as a player, he returned as their coach. Detroit went 33–31–12 under Gadsby in 1968–69 but missed the Stanley Cup Playoffs. They won their first two games of the 1969–70 season under Gadsby, earning congratulations from owner Bruce Norris.

"We were 8–1 in the exhibition games and won the first two in the regular season," Gadsby told the *Toronto Star* in 2000. "Bruce Norris came into the dressing room, put his arm around me, and told me I was doing a hell of a job. Next day he fired me. I never have figured out why."

Alex Delvecchio retired as a player early in the 1973–74 season and immediately went behind the bench. The Red Wings finished 27–31–9 and missed the playoffs. He coached the Red Wings and even added the general manager's job to his portfolio at one point, before leaving in 1977 and becoming a successful businessman.

Though Gordie Howe spent 25 seasons with the Red Wings as a player, he never officially served as coach. Howe retired as a player in 1971, then spent the next two seasons in Detroit's front office before returning to the ice as a player with the Houston Aeros of the World Hockey Association. He returned to the NHL in 1979 with the Hartford Whalers and played one more season before calling it quits for good. He never did officially coach the Red Wings.

11 There's no evidence that Alex Delvecchio was ever overweight, but the Hall of Fame center carried the nickname "Fats" for most of his NHL career because his face had some baby fat when he first entered the NHL. In fact, he looked like an 18 year old well after he had become one of the NHL's top players and a future Hall of Famer.

He retired on November 7, 1973, having played 1,549 regular-season games and finishing with 456 goals and 825 assists for 1,281 points. At the time he called it a career, he ranked second to longtime linemate Gordie Howe in all three categories. He also had 35 goals and 104 points in 121 Stanley Cup Playoff games.

Pavel Datsyuk could do things with the puck most players could only dream of. The "Datsyukian Deke" on breakaways and, especially, shootout attempts became a fixture in the lexicon of Detroit hockey fans. He was a maestro with the puck, a true magician when it came to finding ways to take it away from opponents and keep it away while generating offense.

Datsyuk earned the nickname "Magic Man" after his dazzling performances became the norm. Datsyuk's goals, stickhandles, and passes became consistent highlight-reel material, and his moves routinely hit six figures in views on YouTube. As a true wizard with the puck, the nickname was a perfect fit. Type "Magic Man" into a search engine and you'll see for yourself.

Johan Franzen's nickname came from Steve Yzerman, who dubbed him "Mule" during his rookie season in 2005–06 after the 6-foot-3, 220-pound forward whizzed past him on the ice. Yzerman said he earned it because "he carried the load."

"He's big and strong, and he reminded me of a mule that day," Yzerman told the Canadian Press in 2008. "His offensive game really started to show up last year, and now that his confidence has grown, he is holding onto the puck and making plays."

But it took a little while for Franzen to feel comfortable with the nickname.

"At first, he didn't know what [mule] meant and didn't know if it was a good or a bad thing," defenseman Niklas Kronwall, Franzen's road roomie, said in 2008. "Once he found out what it meant, he was proud of it."

Franzen may have taken a while to realize that "Mule" was actually a compliment, but there was no doubt about Nicklas Lidstrom's nickname being favorable—after all, how many of us wouldn't want to be called "The Perfect Human."

On the ice, Lidstrom was about as close to perfection as a player could be. He won the Norris Trophy seven times—more than anyone except Bobby Orr—was part of four Stanley Cup-winning teams with

Johan Franzen was dubbed "Mule" by Steve Yzerman because "he carried the load." (Michael Miller—Own work; License: CC BY-SA 3.0; Source: https://commons.wikimedia.org/w/index.php?curid=18308610)

the Red Wings, won the Conn Smythe Trophy in 2002, and was the team captain for his last six seasons.

The hardest thing to find was Lidstrom making a mistake, on or off the ice.

"It was Kris Draper and Chris Osgood kind of joking about it, that's how it first came out, and that's how it grew," Lidstrom told MLive.com in 2015, prior to being inducted into the Hockey Hall of Fame. "I took a lot of pride in being prepared for games and practices and tried to play at a high level all the time. But that nickname is something I just chuckle about."

He admitted that the one person who could have crushed that perception was his wife.

"She could have killed that story real quick," he said.

If hockey were an academic subject, you'd want Igor Larionov as your teacher.

Larionov centered one of the great lines in hockey history, the "KLM Line" with Vladimir Krutov and Sergei Makarov, while playing in the Soviet Union. That's where he picked up the nickname "The Professor" a tribute to his incredible vision and ability to read the game, as well as his ultra-intelligent appearance off the ice.

Larionov was 28 when he was allowed to come to North America and join the Vancouver Canucks. When he joined the Red Wings, he was close to 35.

"They called him 'The Professor,' because of his trademark glasses and [because] he was so smart and even-keeled on the ice and off it," former Red Wings defenseman Aaron Ward related to the team's website in 2008. "He played the game with ease and was just always under control. I remember when I'd lose my composure as a young man, he would always tell me, 'Just think the game. Make decisions as carefully as you can and think about how to approach your next move.'

"I mean, here's a guy who was maybe 175 pounds and maybe 5-foot-10, but he was so successful on both the international stage and then in the NHL because he always tried to learn the game and then preach what he learned to the young guys around him. He was, and is, one of the best character guys and smartest people I've met."

12 Playoff games that go multiple overtimes are nothing new. But Game 1 of the Semifinals between the Red Wings and the Montreal Maroons on March 24, 1936, still takes the cake. More than eight decades later, it remains unchallenged as the longest game in NHL history.

The teams entered the series evenly matched. The Red Wings (24–16–8) had won the American Division. The Maroons (22–16–10) had finished first in the Canadian Division. Under the playoff format in use at the time, the division winners got a bye through the Quarterfinals but were matched against each other in the Semifinals; the other series matched the two winners from the Quarterfinals, with the winners advancing to the Stanley Cup Final.

Though each team had plenty of scorers, it wasn't a big surprise that no one was able to get a shot past Detroit goaltender Normie Smith or his Montreal counterpart, Lorne Chabot, through the regulation 60 minutes in the series opener at the Montreal Forum. The zeroes stayed on the scoreboard through the first, second, and third overtimes, with the clock ticking past midnight.

The Zamboni was still more than a decade away from being invented, so the ice deteriorated. By the time the puck dropped for the fourth overtime, the surface was rutted and chewed up, further slowing the game and taking a toll on the skilled players.

Detroit nearly won the game in the fifth overtime when Herbie Lewis went in on a breakaway and beat Chabot. But instead of celebrating a victory, Lewis had to watch the puck clang off the post and away from the net.

Soon after, Montreal had a great chance when Baldy Northcott was set up by Hooley Smith. But to the despair of the crowd, Smith got his pad out and kept the game scoreless.

It was after 2 a.m. when the teams took the ice for the sixth overtime, their *ninth* period of hockey that night. They had already surpassed the NHL record for the longest game, set by the Toronto Maple Leafs and Boston Bruins on April 4, 1932.

With each coach searching for younger legs, Detroit's Jack Adams sent out rookie forward Mud Bruneteau on a line with vets Syd Howe and Hec Kilrea. Bruneteau had seen little action after scoring just twice during the regular season. But after sitting for most of the first eight-plus periods, Bruneteau was one of the few players who still had something in the tank.

The sixth overtime had passed the 16-minute mark when Bruneteau controlled the puck in his own zone and passed it to Kilrea to start a rush. Kilrea faked a pass and slid the puck over the blue line, where Bruneteau, the fastest guy on the chewed-up ice, got past the Montreal defense and picked it up.

He went in one-on-one with Chabot and let fly.

"Thank God," Bruneteau later recalled. "Chabot fell down as I shot the puck into the net. It was the funniest thing: the puck just stuck there in the twine and didn't fall on the ice."

Though the goal judge failed to turn on the red light, referee Bill Stewart signaled it was a goal, and after 116 minutes and 30 seconds of overtime, at 2:25 in the morning, Detroit had a 1–0 victory. Though shots on goal were still two decades away from being an official NHL statistic, Smith reportedly finished with at least 90 saves.

According to hockey historian Stan Fischler, there's one more piece to the story. Bruneteau was back at his hotel room, preparing to undress, when he heard a knock at the door. When he finally answered, there was Chabot.

"Sorry to bother you, kid," the goaltender said, "but you forgot something when you left the rink." Then, handing Bruneteau a puck, said, "Maybe you'd like to have this souvenir of the goal you scored."

The Red Wings went on to sweep the best-of-five series and do the same to the Toronto Maple Leafs in the Final to win the Stanley Cup for the first time in their history,

13 Gordie Howe and Terry Sawchuk might well have won the Conn Smythe Trophy during the Red Wings' run of four championships in six seasons from 1950 to 1955, but the award for playoff MVP hadn't been established yet.

It wasn't until 1965 that the NHL instituted the Conn Smythe, with future Hockey Hall of Famer Jean Beliveau winning the first one after the Montreal Canadiens won their first Cup in five years.

The Canadiens were back in the Final in 1966, this time against the Red Wings. Detroit had finished fourth during the regular season, earning them a meeting with the second-place Chicago Black Hawks.

Chicago had gone 11–1–2 against the Red Wings during the regular season. But behind the play of goaltender Roger Crozier, who allowed 10 goals in the six games, Detroit advanced to the Final against the Canadiens; the regular-season champions had swept the third-place Toronto Maple Leafs in four games.

The Stanley Cup Final opened on April 24, and Crozier continued his superb play by making 33 saves in a 3–2 win at the Forum. Two nights later, Crozier allowed an early power-play goal by J.C. Tremblay, then surrendered just one other goal in a 5–2 win that put the Red Wings in the driver's seat: They led the series, 2–0, and were coming home for Games 3 and 4.

The Red Wings took an early lead in Game 3 when Norm Ullman scored 4:20 into the game, but Montreal scored four unanswered goals and won, 4–2. Game 4 was scoreless early in the first period when Crozier had to leave with a sprained knee and twisted ankle.

"At first, I thought my leg was broken," Crozier said of the play. "I was stretching for the corner of the goal when [Montreal forward Bobby] Rousseau fell going through the crease, jamming my leg against the post. There was a searing pain, and my leg went limp. It started to quiver. I couldn't control it and couldn't regain my feet."

Ullman scored midway through the second period to put Detroit ahead, 1–0, but Beliveau tied the score, 1–1, late in the period against Hank Bassen, and Ralph Backstrom's third-period goal gave Montreal a 2–1 win.

Crozier was back in goal for Game 5, a 5–1 win by the Canadiens at the Forum. The Red Wings rallied from a two-goal deficit to force overtime in Game 6, but Henri Richard scored a disputed goal 2:20 into OT for a 3–2 win that gave the Canadiens the Cup.

Though his team didn't win the Cup that year, Crozier was selected as the playoff MVP. He learned he'd won the award while he was peeling his uniform away from the injured parts of his body in the Wings' dressing room. He changed into his street clothes to accept the trophy from NHL President Clarence Campbell. His body may have still hurt, but Crozier's wallet felt better after he pocketed the $1,000 cash award that came with the Cup, not to mention a sports car.

14 Six players have accounted for the 11 seasons in which a Red Wing has scored 50 or more goals.

By far, the most prolific was Steve Yzerman. He has the three highest-scoring seasons in franchise history: 65 goals in 1999–89, 62 in 1989–90, and 58 in 1992–93. Yzerman also scored 51 goals in 1990–91 and 50 in 1987–88.

Sergei Fedorov (56 in 1993–94), John Ogrodnick (55 in 1984–85), Ray Sheppard (52 in 1993–94), and Danny Grant (50 in 1974–75) had one apiece. Gordie Howe had 49 in a 70-game season (1952–53) and Frank Mahovlich scored 49 in 1968–69, when the season was 76 games.

But the only Red Wing other than Yzerman to score 50 or more goals more than once is probably better known to most of today's Detroit fans for his work on television rather than his play on the ice.

Mickey Redmond was part of the package the Wings received when they traded Mahovlich to the Montreal Canadiens during the 1970–71 season. Redmond was a two-time Stanley Cup winner and had scored 27 goals in 1969–70, but on a team swimming in talented young forwards, Redmond was regarded as expendable.

Mahovlich helped the Canadiens win the Cup in 1971 and 1973, but the Red Wings had to be more than happy with the return. (They got two useful forwards, Bill Collins and Guy Charron, along with Redmond.)

Given a bigger role, Redmond produced 42 goals and 71 points in 1971–72. But that was just a warm-up for the 1972–73 season, in which he set a Red Wings record by scoring 52 goals. He also had 41 assists to finish with 93 points. Then he proved that was no fluke by scoring 51 in 1973–74. That made him just the third player in NHL history, after Bobby Hull and Phil Esposito, to have back-to-back seasons with at least 50 goals.

Redmond was a First-Team NHL All-Star in 1972–73 and a Second-Team All-Star in 1973–74; at age 27, he appeared ready to remain among the NHL's top goal-scorers for several more years. But his time as one of hockey's most feared scorers came to a sudden end early in the 1974–75 season, when a ruptured disc caused permanent damage to a nerve running directly to his right leg.

An operation to repair the problem proved unsuccessful, and Redmond, who would play only parts of his two last seasons in Detroit, called it a career in 1976 at the age of 28.

Today, instead of having become a Red Wings legend as a player, he's become one as a broadcaster, with generations of fans who never saw his years as a 50-goal scorer coming to know him as one of the voices of winter. He never made the playoffs with the Wings as a player, but he was there to describe the exploits of Detroit's four Cup-winning teams from 1997 to 2008.

15 Even in the high-scoring 1980s and early 1990s, 70 assists were a lot. Steve Yzerman set the franchise record when he became the second player in Wings history to exceed that mark, in 1988–89, when he piled up 90, a total no one wearing the winged wheel has come close to. The second-highest total in team history also belongs to Yzerman, who set up 79 goals in 1992–93.

Still, the first Red Wing to break the 70-assist mark did so long before Yzerman put on a Detroit sweater.

The Red Wings selected Marcel Dionne with the No. 2 pick in the 1971 NHL Draft. Though he was generously listed at 5-foot-9 (but was likely shorter), Dionne was a solid 180-pound forward who had put up huge numbers with the St. Catharines Black Hawks of the Ontario Hockey League.

Dionne was a sensation as an NHL rookie, scoring 28 goals and finishing with 77 points, though he ended up just third in the balloting for the Calder Trophy as the NHL's top rookie. He bumped those totals to 40 goals and 90 points in 1972–73 and had 24 goals and 78 points in 1973–74.

By then, the old guard, players such as Gordie Howe and Alex Delvecchio, were gone and Dionne was the team's unquestioned star.

Early in 1974–75, Delvecchio, now the Wings' coach, moved

Marcel Dionne set a Red Wings record with 121 points in 1974–75. (Sean Hagen, Maple Ridge, Canada - DSC_0295; License: CC BY-SA 2.0; Credit: https://commons.wikimedia.org/w/index.php?curid=5260743)

struggling forward Danny Grant onto Dionne's line—and Grant suddenly became a 50-goal scorer. Dionne scored 47 goals—including an NHL-record 10 while Detroit was short-handed—and set franchise records with 74 assists and 121 points. He was awarded the Lady Byng Trophy for gentlemanly and skillful play.

But Dionne's biggest season with the Red Wings was also his last. When his contract ran out, negotiations on a new deal stalled. The Wings advised his agent to shop Dionne around the NHL, and he landed the richest contract in league history: five years at $300,000 annually from the Los Angeles Kings. The teams worked out a compensation agreement, and Dionne was off to LA, where he proved that his last season with the Wings was no fluke.

16 The Red Wings had no trouble scoring during the 1980s, but a leaky defense and inconsistent goaltending kept Detroit from moving into the NHL's elite. After the Wings failed to qualify for the Stanley Cup Playoffs in 1990 following back-to-back first-place finishes in the Norris Division, ownership decided to make a change behind the bench.

Out went Jacques Demers, who had gotten the Wings to the conference final in 1987 and 1988. In his place, the Red Wings hired Bryan Murray, who had coached the Washington Capitals to respectability in the 1980s but had been fired during the 1989–90 season.

The Red Wings hired Murray as coach and general manager, with Jim Devellano bumped up to vice president. The Wings made it back to the playoffs in 1990–91 despite finishing under .500 (34–38–8) but were eliminated in the first round.

The defensive structure Murray brought with him began to yield results as the talent base improved. The 1991–92 team jumped from 76 points to 98 (43–25–12) and finished first in the Norris Division, but they were upset in the second round of the playoffs.

The Wings improved again in 1992–93, finishing with 103 points (47–24–9), although they came in second in the Norris.

All that meant nothing in the playoffs, and the Wings failed to get out of the first round. Detroit won the first two games of its series against the fourth-place Toronto Maple Leafs, but Toronto won the next three. The Wings rolled to a 7–3 win in Game 6 at Maple Leaf Gardens, but with a chance to win Game 7 on home ice, the Red Wings couldn't hold a 3–2 lead in the final three minutes of the third period. Toronto's Nikolai Borschevsky scored the series-winner at 2:35 of OT to end the Red Wings' season.

That was the end of Murray's tenure behind the bench. The Red Wings hired Scotty Bowman as coach, with Murray remaining as GM. After another disappointing first-round loss following a first-place finish in the Central Division, Murray left the GM's post as well to join the Florida Panthers, with Devellano returning to the general manager's position.

17 Mike Vernon was one of the NHL's most successful goaltenders in the late 1980s and early 1990s with the Calgary Flames. He helped get the Flames to the Stanley Cup Final in 1986, and three years later earned all 16 wins when Calgary capped a spectacular season by avenging their loss to the Montreal Canadiens in the Final three years earlier.

The Flames failed to repeat in 1990, and the team selected goaltender Trevor Kidd in the first round of the 1990 NHL Draft with the idea that he would become Vernon's replacement. After the Flames finished first in the Pacific Division during the regular season, they were upset by the Vancouver Canucks in the opening round of the playoffs, with Vernon going 3–4.

Kidd played 31 games in 1993–94, and the Flames felt he was ready to handle the starting job. That made Vernon expendable. The Red Wings, who were coming off a stunning first-round upset by the San Jose Sharks, felt they needed to make a change as well. The result: On June 29, 1994, the Red Wings traded defenseman Steve Chiasson to the Flames for Vernon.

Vernon got most of the starts in the lockout-shortened 1994–95 season, going 19–6–4 and helping the Red Wings win the Presidents' Trophy as the top team in the regular season. With Vernon carrying the load in goal, the Red Wings advanced to the Stanley Cup Final for the first time since 1966, only to be swept by the New Jersey Devils.

After some cantankerous negotiations, Vernon and the Red Wings agreed on a two-year contract. But he played just 32 games in 1995–96, with youngster Chris Osgood getting more playing time. When Vernon did play, he was superb, finishing 21–7–2 with a 2.26 goals-against average for a team that set an NHL single-season record for wins and led the NHL with 131 points. But Vernon played just four games during the playoffs, going 2–2 before the Wings were eliminated by the Colorado Avalanche in the Western Conference Final.

Vernon was Osgood's backup for most of 1996–97, going 13–11–8 during the regular season. But Osgood struggled down the stretch, and coach Scotty Bowman announced that he would be going with Vernon in the playoffs.

The move worked better than anyone could have dreamed. Vernon went 16–4 with a 1.76 goals-against average, helping the Red Wings end a 42-year drought with their first Stanley Cup championship since 1955.

Unfortunately, the Red Wings then found themselves in a position in which they were likely to lose a goaltender in the NHL Waiver Draft. Rather than lose Vernon for nothing, they traded him to the San Jose Sharks for draft picks on August 18, 1997.

18 In addition to his performance on the ice, Ted Lindsay's NHL legacy includes his work helping to organize the NHL Players' Association. His willingness to take a stand and try to improve the lot of NHL players took a toll on his career (he was still among the league's elite players when he was exiled to the Chicago Black Hawks in 1957), so it's appropriate that the NHLPA's award for the most outstanding player in the regular season, which was established in 1971 as the Lester B. Pearson Award, was renamed in his honor in 2010.

Two Red Wings have taken home the trophy.

Though NHL voters named Wayne Gretzky of the Los Angeles Kings as winner of the Hart Trophy, given to the league's most valuable player, Detroit's Steve Yzerman was voted as the NHL's outstanding player by his fellow players in 1989 (when the award was still the Lester B. Pearson). Yzerman had had his greatest offensive season, finishing with 65 goals, 90 assists, and 155 points, finishing third in all three categories. He led the NHL in even-strength goals with 45 and in shots on goal with 388. He was third in balloting for the Hart Trophy, but first in the voting among his fellow players.

Yzerman inadvertently had a hand in the Red Wings' other winner. He missed nearly one-third of the 1993–94 season with injuries, giving Sergei Fedorov a chance to play top-line minutes. Fedorov took the opportunity and ran with it, finishing with 56 goals, 64 assists,

120 points, and a plus-48 rating to help the Red Wings finish first in the Central Division.

Yzerman was among those who were impressed by Fedorov's performance.

"I've only seen two other players that can dominate a game like Sergei, and that's Wayne and Mario," he said, referring to Gretzky and Lemieux. "In my opinion, he's the best player in the League. He is different than Wayne and Mario, because he dominates with his speed and unbelievable one-on-one moves."

Unlike Yzerman five years earlier, Fedorov in 1994 won both the Hart and the Pearson (now Lindsay) awards, capping off a truly remarkable breakout season.

19 The 1999–2000 season was Steve Yzerman's 17th in the NHL, and, not surprisingly for a player of his caliber and career length, it contained three major milestones, all of which he reached during a nine-day span in late November.

Yzerman scored his 599th goal and earned his 900th assist on November 17, 1999, when the Red Wings extended their unbeaten streak to five games by defeating the Vancouver Canucks. He became the 10th player in NHL history to have 900 assists, and the two-point night increased his career total to 1,499, eighth on the all-time list.

Point number 1,500 came three nights later, when he had an assist on a goal by defenseman Mathieu Dandenault in a 2–1 road loss to the Edmonton Oilers.

Yzerman became the 11th player in NHL history to reach the 600-goal mark when he scored during the Red Wings' 4–2 win against the Oilers at Joe Louis Arena on November 26, 1999.

It wasn't exactly a thing of beauty. Yzerman took a pass from Nicklas Lidstrom, skated along the goal line, and lifted a shot that bounced off the back of goalie Tommy Salo's leg and into the net.

"I just picked up a loose puck," Yzerman said. "Ideally, I would have drawn it up a little prettier than that. But I've gotten some lousy goals over the years, too."

Yzerman joined Wayne Gretzky, Gordie Howe, Marcel Dionne,

and Mark Messier as the only NHL players at the time with 600 goals and 900 assists.

All in all, a pretty good month.

Yzerman finished the season with 75 career game-winning goals and would get 19 more before he retired in 2006.

20 Perhaps the most amazing thing about Nicklas Lidstrom winning the Norris Trophy seven times is that the first one didn't come until he had passed his 30th birthday; he was 31 by the time he actually received the trophy. In comparison, Bobby Orr, the all-time leader in winning the Norris Trophy with eight, had retired a few months after his 30th birthday because of knee injuries.

Lidstrom was an NHL First-Team All-Star in each of the three seasons before 2000–01, when he won the Norris for the first time. He finished with 15 goals and 71 points in 82 games, averaging 28:27 of ice time. He was also voted a First-Team All-Star for the fourth straight season, and, for the third season in a row, he was the runner-up for the Lady Byng Trophy.

Though Lidstrom's offensive numbers were down in 2001–02 (nine goals, 59 points), he was again the engine that made the Red Wings go—this time, all the way to their third Stanley Cup in six seasons. He averaged 28:49 of ice time in 78 games and added to his hardware haul by winning the Conn Smythe Trophy as playoff MVP.

Lidstrom made it three in a row in 2002–03, finishing with 18 goals, 62 points, and a plus-40 rating while averaging a career-high 29:20 of ice time—meaning he was on the ice for almost half the game, every game. He was also chosen a First-Team All-Star for the sixth straight season.

After a subpar (for him) season in 2003–04 and a lockout that canceled the 2004–05 season, Lidstrom began another run of three straight Norris Trophy wins in 2005–06. He finished with a career-high 80 points (16 goals, 64 assists), was plus-21, and averaged 28:07 of ice time—at age 35.

He won again in 2006–07 after finishing with 62 points (13 goals, 49 assists) and another plus-40 rating while averaging 27:29 of

Only Bobby Orr won the Norris Trophy more often than Nicklas Lidstrom. (By Michael Miller—Own work; License: CC BY-SA 3.0; Source: https://commons .wikimedia.org/w/index.php?curid=18250480)

ice time. Norris number six came in 2007–08, when he scored 10 goals and had 70 points as well as a plus-40 rating. He was voted a First-Team All-Star for the ninth time.

In each of the next two seasons, Lidstrom had to settle for being a Second-Team NHL All-Star. He was third in the Norris balloting in 2008–09 and fourth in 2009–10. But despite finishing with a minus-2 rating in 2010–11 (the only time in his NHL career he wasn't a "plus" player), Lidstrom equaled Doug Harvey by winning the Norris for the seventh time. He finished with 16 goals and 62 points while averaging 23:28 of ice time—pretty good for a 40-year-old.

Lidstrom retired after one more season. He finished fifth in the

Norris balloting after putting up 34 points (11 goals, 23 assists) and a plus-21 rating in 70 games.

21 The Lady Byng Trophy actually predates the Wings' arrival in the NHL. It was donated to the league by Evelyn Byng, wife of Canada's governor general at the time, and was to be given to the player "adjudged to have exhibited the best type of sportsmanship and gentlemanly conduct combined with a high standard of playing ability."

The award was first given to Frank Nighbor of the Ottawa Senators after the 1924–25 season. New York Rangers center Frank Boucher won it so often—seven times in eight seasons from 1927–35—that he was actually given permanent custody of the original trophy and a new one was made.

Forward Marty Barry was the first member of the Red Wings to win the award, in 1937, after finishing with six penalty minutes in 47 games (the NHL season at the time was just 48 games).

No Red Wing won the Lady Byng again until 1949, when Bill Quackenbush became the first defenseman to win the award. Quackenbush, a member of the Hockey Hall of Fame, became the second winner to go through a whole season, 60 games in 1948–49, without taking a single penalty. But Quackenbush was more than just a gentlemanly player. He finished the season with six goals and 23 points and was named a First-Team NHL All-Star for the second straight season.

Despite all that, Quackenbush found himself elsewhere before the 1949–50 season began. On August 29, 1949, he was sent to the Boston Bruins in a six-player trade. One of those players, Pete Babando, scored one of the most famous goals in NHL history, the double-OT tally that won the 1950 Stanley Cup.

Quackenbush played seven seasons for the Bruins before retiring, finishing in the top four in voting for the Lady Byng three times.

Two years later, another Red Wings defenseman began a run in which he won the Lady Byng three times in four years.

Red Kelly joined the Wings as a 20 year old in 1947–48 and was an instant hit as a smooth-skating, puck-moving defenseman. He was often partnered with Quackenbush. A Second-Team All-Star and the Lady

Byng runner-up in 1950, he then had an even better season in 1950–51, finishing with 54 points (17 goals, 37 assists) and 24 penalty minutes to earn a berth on the First All-Star team and win the Lady Byng.

"Joe Primeau had trained me very well," Kelly said years later, referring to his junior coach, "so when I went to the NHL, I had been taught the things I should have been taught and I didn't have to learn them when I went up there."

One of those things he learned was that you can't contribute from the penalty box. In his three Lady Byng seasons, he took a combined total of 50 penalty minutes.

Kelly was a First-Team All-Star and the Lady Byng runner-up in 1952, then won the trophy again in 1953 and 1954 while again earning a First-Team All-Star berth. In 1954, he also became the first winner of the Norris Trophy, a new award given to the NHL's top defenseman.

22 Gordie Howe led the Red Wings and the NHL in scoring for four consecutive seasons. from 1950–51 through 1953–54, before finishing second on the team to Dutch Reibel in 1954–55.

But Howe was back on top in scoring among the Red Wings in 1955–56, piling up 38 goals and 79 points in a 70-game season. From then until 1969–70, Howe won two more NHL scoring titles, finished in the top five in the league in scoring every season, and led the Red Wings in points 13 times.

Howe had at least 72 points (in a 70-game season) and led the Wings in scoring for nine consecutive seasons, when he finished second to a young center named Norm Ullman.

Ullman joined the Wings in 1955–56 and soon became one of the NHL's most consistently productive players. He had seven straight 20-goal seasons and put up at least 50 points in eight consecutive seasons through 1963–64.

In 1964–65, Ullman had a career year. He went from 21 goals to 41 and from 51 points to 83. That put him ahead of Howe, who had 29 goals and 76 points. Ullman was second in the NHL in scoring behind Chicago's Stan Mikita (87 points); Howe came in third.

Howe finished first on the Wings in scoring in 1965–66, but, in 1966–67, Ullman again finished ahead of Howe with 70 points, five more than Howe. Ullman finished third in the NHL in scoring behind Chicago teammates Mikita (97 points) and Bobby Hull (80), while Howe tied for fourth with another Black Hawk, Kenny Wharram.

Ullman had 30 goals and 55 points through 58 games in 1967–68 when he was sent to the Toronto Maple Leafs in one of the biggest trades in NHL history. He finished the season with a combined total of 35 goals and 72 points; Howe led the Wings with 39 goals and 82 points.

Howe led the Wings in scoring in each of the next two seasons, before finishing with 52 points in 1970–71, his final season in Detroit.

23 Even in today's NHL, where games no longer end in ties, 40 wins are a lot. In the past 70 years, three Red Wings goaltenders won as many as 40 games once: Roger Crozier, who won 40 in 1964–65, and Dominik Hasek, who had 41 victories in 2001–02 before helping the Red Wings win the Stanley Cup.

Chris Osgood came close with 39 wins in 1995–96; Hasek (2006–07) and Tim Cheveldae (1991–92) each won 38. Glenn Hall also had 38 wins, his coming in 1955–56.

But the only Detroit goaltender to finish a season with 40 or more victories more than once is Terry Sawchuk, who did it three times in a span of five seasons beginning in 1950–51.

Detroit entered that season as the defending Stanley Cup champion. But the Wings also had a new starting goaltender. Though they'd won the Cup the previous spring with Harry Lumley between the pipes, Sawchuk had been impressive during a seven-game call-up during January 1950 while Lumley was injured. GM Jack Adams traded Lumley to the Chicago Black Hawks during the offseason, and the Wings entered the season with an untested rookie goaltender. But Sawchuk was every bit as good as the Red Wings could have hoped for—and more.

Sawchuk played every minute of the 1950–51 season and set an NHL for victories by winning 44 games. He went 44–13–13 with a

1.97 goals-against average and 11 shutouts, helping the Red Wings finish first in the regular season. He won the Vezina Trophy, then given to the goaltender on the team that allowed the fewest goals, as well as the Calder Trophy as the NHL's top rookie.

If there were any doubts that his rookie season was no fluke, Sawchuk dispelled them by matching his own single-season record for victories by winning 44 games in 1951–52, again helping the Red Wings win the Prince of Wales Trophy, then given to the regular-season champion. He was 44–14–12 with a 1.90 GAA and 12 shutouts.

Unlike 1950–51, when the Red Wings were upset in the Semifinals, the 1951–52 season ended with another Stanley Cup championship. Had there been a Conn Smythe Trophy awarded at the time, Sawchuk would probably been a shoo-in: He allowed five goals in eight games (0.63 GAA) and had four shutouts.

Sawchuk's goals-against average was below 2.00 in each of the next two seasons and he led the NHL in victories, but he won "only" 32 games in 1952–53 and 35 in 1953–54.

His third 40-win season came in 1954–55. Sawchuk went 40–17–11 with a 1.96 GAA and 12 shutouts (the third time in four seasons he'd had a dozen). He capped the season by going 8–3 in the playoffs, helping the Red Wings win the Cup for the fourth time in six seasons.

But just as Sawchuk's promise had persuaded the Wings to trade away a Cup-winning goaltender in Lumley, the Red Wings were enamored of backup Glenn Hall and felt Sawchuk was expendable. He was traded to the Boston Bruins on June 3, 1955. Though Hall did end up being as good as the Wings had hoped, they didn't win the Stanley Cup in his two seasons as the starter, and Detroit reacquired Sawchuk in July 1957. Sawchuk played in the NHL until 1970, but never won more than 29 games in a season again.

24 It's a hard concept to grasp now, but in the Original Six era, most teams carried just one goaltender. The home team might have a spare goalie, sometimes a team trainer, sometimes a minor leaguer, on hand if either goaltender got hurt during a game. But basically, a team carried one goaltender who was expected to play as many games as possible, including back-to-backs, three games in four nights, etc.

By the time Dominik Hasek joined the Wings in 2001, there was no expectation that a goaltender would play every game. Hasek's 65 games were a little above the norm for a top-flight starting goaltender. But with 41 wins and a 2.17 goals-against average, it proved to be the perfect workload to have him ready for the Stanley Cup Playoffs, when he led the Wings to their third championship in six seasons.

The last Detroit goaltender to play in every game during a season was Roger Crozier, who appeared in all 70 games during 1964–65—but Crozier didn't finish all of them. Crozier was 40–22–7 and played 4,166 of a possible 4,200 minutes. Carl Wetzel, a longtime minor league goaltender, got into two games and was the loser in relief against the Montreal Canadiens on December 26, 1964, allowing four goals on 18 shots.

Glenn Hall literally never missed a minute during his two seasons with the Red Wings. He started all 70 games and played 4,200 minutes in 1955–56 and 1956–57 after taking over the starting job when the Wings traded Terry Sawchuk to the Boston Bruins. He went 68–44–28 during that span.

Sawchuk played every minute of the Red Wings' 70 games in 1950–51, and again in 1952, winning 44 games each time and posting a goals-against average below 2.00 each time. He played 63, 67, and 68 games in the next three seasons with the Wings, again finishing with a GAA below 2.00.

The Red Wings brought Sawchuk back in 1957, two years after they had traded him to the Boston Bruins for Johnny Bucyk. Sawchuk matched Hall in terms of showing up for work every night, starting and finishing all 70 games. However, the magic he'd had in his first stint with the Wings wasn't there. He finished the 1957–58 season 29–29–12 with a 2.94 goals-against average.

No Detroit goaltender since then has played every minute of every game—and given the longer schedule and travel of today's NHL, it's safe to say no one ever will.

25 The Red Wings reached double figures in goals for first time by holding a Christmas party, with the Toronto Maple Leafs as the unwilling guests. The Wings routed the Leafs, 10–1, at the Olympia on December 25, 1930.

The first road game in which the Red Wings reached double figures took place on December 13, 1934, when the Wings pummeled the St. Louis Eagles, 11–2. It was the only NHL season for the Eagles, who had relocated from Ottawa and folded after 1934–35.

The Wings had one double-figure night each in 1941–42 and 1942–43, then had three in each of the following two seasons. That included the biggest shutout win in NHL history, a 15–0 demolition of the New York Rangers on January 23, 1944. It was one of five times in a span of three seasons that the Wings scored 10 goals or more against the Rangers.

The Red Wings hit double figures three times during the 1952–53 season, the last on March 2, 1953, when they routed the Boston Bruins, 10–2, at the Olympia. That was their last 10-plus goal game until March 18, 1965, when they drubbed Boston, 10–3.

Detroit reached double figures just once more in the 1960s and twice in the 1970s, but then did it 12 times in a span of 15 seasons from 1981–82 through 1995–96. Among those games was a 12–0 victory against the Chicago Blackhawks on December 4, 1987, the biggest margin of victory for the Wings during their time at Joe Louis Arena.

The Red Wings haven't reached double figures in a home game since November 27, 1993, when they defeated the Dallas Stars, 10–4. They won, 10–3, at the San Jose Sharks on January 6, 1994, the fourth time they had scored 10 or more goals in a road game.

The last time Detroit hit double figures on the road was December 2, 1995, when they embarrassed the Montreal Canadiens, 11–1, at the Forum. Slava Kozlov scored three times for the Wings, who had nine times on 26 shots against Patrick Roy before the furious goaltender was removed. (Roy never played for the Canadiens again and was dealt to the Colorado Avalanche a few days later.)

Since then, the Red Wings have allowed 10 goals in a game twice.

They lost, 10–3, to the St. Louis Blues at Joe Louis Arena on March 30, 2010, and 10–1 to the Canadiens at Montreal on December 2, 2017.

26 Few defensemen score three goals in an NHL game. Nicklas Lidstrom, a first-ballot Hall of Famer, did it exactly once in his career, on December 15, 2010, against the St. Louis Blues.

Since the NHL's first expansion in 1967, three players have accounted for the five hat tricks scored by Red Wings defenseman.

When Lidstrom got his, he was the first Detroit defenseman to score three goals in a game since Reed Larson had done it on February 27, 1985, when he got three in an 11–5 victory against the Vancouver Canucks. Larson had scored three times in a game twice before, each in a road game against the Pittsburgh Penguins, the first in a 6–4 loss on January 3, 1981, and again in a 7–3 win on February 15, 1983.

But the most recent hat trick by a Red Wings defenseman belongs to Mike Green, who scored three times in a 5–1 win against the Ottawa Senators at Joe Louis Arena on October 17, 2016.

Green was a prolific offensive contributor for most of the first decade of his NHL career while playing for the Washington Capitals. He's the last defenseman to score 30 goals in a season (31 in 2008–09) and had back-to-back 70-point seasons in 2008–09 (76) and 2009–10 (73).

Green scored his first goal of the 2016–17 season when he wired a wrist shot over the shoulder of Senators goaltender Andrew Hammond at 11:43 of the first period, giving Detroit a 1–0 lead. After Darren Helm made it 2–0 at 14:15, Green got his second of the game at 17:17, slipping down from the point into the high slot and one-timing a pass from Thomas Vanek past a screened Hammond.

After Ottawa's Ryan Dzingel scored the only goal of the second period to make it 3–1, Green completed his hat trick at 13:24 of the third period. Riley Sheahan won a puck battle in the right corner, and Luke Glendening fed Green at the right point. Green took advantage of some open space to drift into the high slot and beat Hammond with a wrist shot through traffic, setting off a cascade of hats onto the ice.

Green finished the 2016–17 season with 14 goals, the most he'd scored in one season since getting 19 with the Capitals in 2009–10.

27 The Red Wings qualified for the Stanley Cup Playoffs for the first time in 1928–29, their third season in the NHL. They finished third in the American Division with a 19–16–9 record, the first time they finished over .500. That earned the Wings a first-round series against the Toronto Maple Leafs, who had finished third in the Canadian Division. Each team finished the season with 52 points, but the Leafs disposed of the Wings easily, winning, 3–1, in Detroit and 4–1 at Toronto to take the total-goals series, 7–2.

It took the Wings three years to get back into the playoffs. Detroit finished fourth in 1929–30 and 1930–31. The Red Wings were below .500 again in 1931–32 but ended up third in the four-team American Division with a record of 18–20–10. They played the Montreal Maroons, who had finished third in the Canadian Division, in the first round, but again came up short in a total-goals series. The teams played to a 1–1 tie on March 29, but Detroit lost, 2–0, in Montreal two nights later, giving the Maroons a 3–1 victory.

The 1932–33 season was the most successful in team history to that point. The Red Wings finished 25–15–8, tying the Boston Bruins for first place in the American Division (the Bruins finished first on tiebreakers). The Maroons, second in the Canadian Division, were again Detroit's opponent in the Quarterfinals, a two-game, total-goals series—but this time the result was different.

The series opened in Montreal on March 25, 1933, and Detroit goaltender John Ross Roach was perfect. Goals by Larry Aurie and Carl Voss were more than enough support in a 2–0 victory that gave the Wings their first victory in a playoff game.

Three nights later at the Olympia, the Maroons jumped to a 2–0 lead when Hooley Smith scored twice midway through the second period. But Herbie Lewis got one goal back in the final seconds of the second period, Ebbie Goodfellow tied the game, 2–2, at 3:47 of the second period, and John Gallagher's goal with 4:06 remaining gave Detroit a 3–2 win and a 5–2 margin in goals.

The Wings came up short in the Semifinals against the New York Rangers, losing, 2–0, in New York on March 30 and 4–3 at the Olympia three nights later.

28 Gordie Howe played 1,687 games with the Red Wings, the most in franchise history. However, his return to the NHL with the Hartford Whalers removed him from the list of players who've played 1,500 or more NHL games and spent their entire career with one team. Howe does hold the league record for games played with 1,767; the final 80 came with the Whalers in 1979–80.

Entering the 2018–19 season, 18 players have played 1,500 or more regular-season games in the NHL. Three of the four who spent their entire careers with one team did so with the Red Wings; five more members of the 1,500-game club spent parts of their careers with Detroit.

Defenseman Nicklas Lidstrom is 12th on the all-time list with 1,564 games played, but he holds the NHL record for games played in a career spent with one team. Lidstrom, Detroit's third-round pick in the 1989 NHL Draft, made his NHL debut in 1991–92, finishing with 60 points (11 goals, 49 assists), while playing in all 80 games.

Lidstrom played every game in each of the next two seasons and didn't miss a game until 1994–95, when he played 43 of 48 games in a lockout-shortened season. For the next 11 seasons, Lidstrom didn't miss more than three games in any season. He played 76 of the 82 games in 2007–08 and 2008–09, then played in all 82 games in each of the following two seasons. Not until 2011–12, his final season, did Lidstrom miss more than six games, playing 70 of Detroit's 82 games.

Like Lidstrom, Alex Delvecchio was both skilled and durable. He made his debut by playing one game in the 1950–51 season, became an NHL regular the following season, and remained one until retiring after playing 11 games in 1973–74, giving him 1,549 during a career that earned him induction into the Hockey Hall of Fame.

Delvecchio played 65 of 70 games in 1951–52, his first full NHL season, and missed a total of two games in the next four seasons. After being limited to 48 games in 1956–57, Delvecchio played all 70 games in each of the next seven seasons. He missed two games in 1964–65, then played every game in each of the next three seasons.

Even as he entered his late thirties, Delvecchio remained among the NHL's most durable players. He missed no more than five games in any of his last five full seasons and played the first 11 games in 1973–74 before retiring and stepping behind the bench as coach.

Steve Yzerman played each of his 1,514 NHL games in a Red Wings jersey. Yzerman, the fourth player selected in the 1983 NHL Draft, played all 80 games in each of his first two NHL seasons before missing 29 in 1985–86.

Unlike Lidstrom and Delvecchio, Yzerman did miss substantial chunks of time during his 22 seasons in Detroit. He missed 16 games in 1987–88 and 26 in 1993–94. From 2000–01 through 2002–03, Yzerman played just 122 of a possible 246 games; he was limited to 16 games in 2002–03 because of knee surgery. Yzerman rebounded by playing 75 of 82 games in 2003–04 and dressed for 61 of 82 games in 2005–06, including his 1,500th on March 15, 2006.

29 The Red Wings were helped by playing in the NHL's weakest division, the Norris, in 1986–87 and 1987–88. Under new coach Jacques Demers, the Wings rebounded from a last-place finish in 1985–86 to finish second in 1986–87 by going 34–36–10 for 78 points, one behind the first-place St. Louis Blues.

Under the playoff structure then in use, the first two rounds were played within the division, with the division champions facing off for the conference title and the conference winners playing for the Stanley Cup.

In 1987, that meant the Red Wings opened the playoffs against the third-place Chicago Blackhawks. The Wings opened the series with 3–1 and 5–1 wins at Joe Louis Arena, took Game 3 at Chicago Stadium when Shawn Burr scored in overtime for a 4–3 victory, then completed the sweep with a 3–1 win and their first playoff series victory in 21 years.

The Norris Division Final matched the Red Wings and the fourth-place Toronto Maple Leafs, who had upset the first-place Blues in the division semifinals. Toronto stunned the crowd at Joe Louis Arena by winning the first two games, 4–2, and 7–2. Detroit won, 4–2, in Game 3 at Maple Leaf Gardens, but Mike Allison's overtime goal gave Toronto a 3–2 win and a 3–1 series lead.

The Red Wings regrouped before Game 5 and extended the series when Glen Hanlon kept the Leafs off the board in a 3–0 win. Detroit won, 4–2, at Toronto in Game 6, and Hanlon pitched another 3–0 shutout in Game 7.

With the Norris Division title in hand, the Red Wings faced the Smythe Division winners, the Edmonton Oilers, in the Campbell Conference Final. The Oilers had finished with an NHL-best 106 points during the regular season, but the Wings stunned the crowd at Northlands Coliseum with a 3–1 win in the opener.

That was as far as they got. Edmonton won the next four games, limiting the Red Wings to five goals, then won the Cup by outlasting the Philadelphia Flyers in a seven-game Final.

In 1987–88, the Wings won the Norris with a 41–28–11 record. The 93 points were the most they had amassed in one season since getting 95 in 1969–70. They lost the first game of their division semifinal against Toronto at home but rebounded to win in six games. Detroit then defeated St. Louis in five games to win the division playoff title for the second straight season and earn a rematch with the Oilers in the Campbell Conference Final.

The Red Wings lost the first two games in Edmonton, then won, 5–2, in Game 3 at Joe Louis Arena. But Edmonton's Jari Kurri scored 11:02 into overtime for a 4–3 win in Game 4, and the Oilers got their offense rolling in Game 5, winning, 8–4, to eliminate the Wings one step from the Stanley Cup for the second straight year. Edmonton retained the Cup by defeating the Boston Bruins in the Final.

30 Nicklas Lidstrom is eighth on the list for all-time plus/minus at plus-450 (the NHL calculates plus/minus ratings as far back as 1959–60). He was a plus player for 19 of his 20 NHL seasons, was plus-11 or better in 17 of those, and plus-40 or better four times.

Lidstrom broke into the NHL in 1991–92 and was the Calder Trophy runner-up after finishing with 11 goals and 60 points as well as a plus-36 rating. That was third in the NHL behind two of his Detroit teammates, forward Paul Ysebaert (plus-44) and defenseman Brad McCrimmon (plus-39).

After finishing plus-7 in 1992–93, Lidstrom had a career-best plus-43 rating in 1993–94, He was in double figures in plus/minus ratings in each of the next six seasons before dropping to plus-9 in 2000–01, when he won the Norris Trophy as the NHL's top defenseman for the first time.

Lidstrom had a plus-13 rating in 2001–02, when he repeated as winner of the Norris Trophy. He was plus-40 in 2002–03, a rating he matched in 2005–06 and 2006–07, when he won the Norris for the fifth and sixth times.

After going plus-31 in 2008–09 and plus-22 in 2009–10, Lidstrom had his only minus season in 2010–11, finishing at minus-2. That didn't discourage voters from selecting him for his seventh and final Norris Trophy and his 10th First-Team All-Star nod.

Lidstrom went plus-21 in 2010–11, his final season.

31 The Red Wings finished the 1995–96 season with a franchise-record 131 points, one shy of the NHL record set by the Montreal Canadiens in 1976–77. But they had to work harder than expected before defeating the Winnipeg Jets in the Western Conference Quarterfinals.

The eighth-seeded Jets lost three of the first four games, then won Game 5 in Detroit before the Wings wrapped up a six-game series victory with a 4–1 win in Winnipeg. It was the Jets' final game at Winnipeg Arena before they moved to Phoenix for the 1996–97 season.

That moved the Wings into the Western Conference Semifinals, where they faced the St. Louis Blues. St. Louis had finished 51 points behind Detroit in the Central Division, but they knocked off the Toronto Maple Leafs in their conference quarterfinal and were confident they could pull off one of the biggest upsets in NHL history.

To no one's surprise, the Red Wings won the first two games of the series. In front of packed houses at Joe Louis Arena, Detroit won the opener, 3–1, and rolled to an 8–3 win in Game 2.

But the Blues refused to roll over. Igor Kravchuk's goal at 3:23 of OT gave St. Louis a 5–4 win in Game 3, and Jon Casey shut out the Wings, 1–0, in Game 4 to even the series.

St. Louis took its first lead in the series and stunned the full house at Joe Louis Arena with a 3–2 win in Game 5. But Detroit rebounded with a 4–2 win at St. Louis in Game 6, setting up a winner-take-all Game 7 back at the Joe.

The Red Wings failed to convert on three power plays in the scoreless first period, when Detroit had a 14–4 margin in shots on goal. The Blues had the better of play in the second, outshooting the Wings, 11–6, in another scoreless period. Neither team scored in the third period, and the Blues outshot the Red Wings, 8–6, in the first overtime. However, neither Casey nor Detroit's Chris Osgood blinked, and the game remained scoreless through 80 minutes and four hours of play.

Then up stepped Steve Yzerman.

Detroit's captain picked up a puck that bounced off Wayne Gretzky's stick in the Detroit zone and raced the other way. Just after crossing the St. Louis blue line, he wound up and drilled a long slap shot that beat Casey, giving Detroit a 1–0 win and moving the Red Wings into the Western Conference Final.

"I couldn't believe it went in," Yzerman said. "I don't score a whole lot of goals from out there. To score a goal in overtime, particularly in Game 7, is a tremendous thrill. Every player dreams of that.

"We really proved to ourselves how to approach tough games and tough situations. If anything, our attitude got better, our will got stronger, and our confidence grew."

32 The Red Wings used four goaltenders during the 1943–44 season, with Connie Dion seeing the most action (26 games). But 17-year-old Harry Lumley also got to play two games, and though he lost both while allowing 13 goals, he made enough of an impression to get a chance to win the starting job in 1944–45.

Lumley, who turned 18 on November 11, 1944, played 37 of Detroit's 50 games, going 24–10–2 with a 3.22 goals-against average and three shutouts in a high-scoring era.

By 1945–46, Lumley was the unquestioned starter. He actually played every minute of all 50 games, going 20–20–10 with a 3.18 GAA and two shutouts. He played in 52 of Detroit's 60 games in 1946–47, then started every game for the next two seasons.

The NHL went to a 70-game schedule in 1949–50, and Lumley played 63 of them. He was 34–19–7 with a 2.35 GAA and seven shutouts. Lumley also played all 14 of Detroit's games on the way to winning the Stanley Cup, going 8–6 with a 1.85 GAA and three shutouts.

But the end of Lumley's time in Detroit was already visible in the distance.

When he was injured in January 1950, the Red Wings brought up a promising young goaltender named Terry Sawchuk, who was on his way to a third straight 30-win season with Indianapolis of the American Hockey League. Sawchuk played seven games, going 4–3–0 with a 2.29 GAA before Lumley returned and reclaimed his job.

On July 13, 1950, the Red Wings cleared the way for Sawchuk by sending Lumley to the Chicago Black Hawks as part of a nine-player trade. Lumley also played with the Toronto Maple Leafs and Boston Bruins before retiring in 1960. He was elected to the Hockey Hall of Fame in 1980.

Sawchuk showed why GM Jack Adams was so willing to trade Lumley by putting together perhaps the best five-season performance in NHL history. From 1950–51 through 1954–55, Sawchuk was 195–78–65 with a 1.94 GAA and 56 shutouts. He led the Wings to the Cup in 1952, 1954, and 1955.

Then, just as he had done five years earlier, Adams decided to change goaltenders. Sawchuk was traded to Boston to make room for Glenn Hall, who had impressed in two games with the Wings in 1954–55.

Hall's numbers weren't what Sawchuk had been putting up, but they were still pretty good. He played every minute of every game during the next two seasons, Hall was 68–44–48 with a 2.16 GAA and 16 shutouts, including 12 in 1956–57.

The one thing Hall couldn't do was win the Stanley Cup. The Red Wings lost the 1956 Final to the Montreal Canadiens, then were upset in the 1957 Semifinals after finishing first in the regular season.

The Wings reacquired Sawchuk from the Bruins in July 1957, sending future Hall of Fame forward Johnny Bucyk to Boston. With Sawchuk back in the fold, they sent Hall and Ted Lindsay to Chicago 13 days later.

Sawchuk stayed with the Red Wings through 1963–64, though he frequently battled injuries and wasn't able to put up the numbers he had during his first stint with the Wings. The Red Wings made him available in the 1964 waiver draft, and Toronto snatched him up. Sawchuk and Johnny Bower formed one of the oldest goaltending duos in NHL history, but they helped the Maple Leafs win the Cup in 1964 and 1967.

Roger Crozier carried the load in goal in 1964–65, starting all 70 games in the first season since World War II that the Red Wings didn't have a Hall of Famer as their No. 1 goaltender.

33 The NHL awarded Detroit a franchise in 1926, on condition the new team had an arena ready for the start of the season. That arena didn't end up coming to fruition in time, and so the Detroit Cougars, the future Red Wings, spent their first season across the river in Windsor, Ontario, at the Border Cities Arena.

Finally, on May 8, 1927, the cornerstone for a new arena was laid at the corner of Detroit's Grand River Avenue and McGraw Street. The building was conceived as an arena strictly for hockey, but with Detroit's economy booming, officials soon came up with a much more extensive project to deal with a quickly expanding convention business.

"Olympia—a Detroit monument to civic pride—will be thrown open to the public for the first time Saturday," the *Detroit News* wrote on October 24, 1927. "Although the new arena . . . was originally planned as a home for the Detroit Hockey Club, later plans have made it a focal point for sporting events and spectacles of the entire state. . . . Detroit now has a place for public events that ranks among the best in the world, well-equipped for boxing shows, pageants, conventions and theatrical spectacles."

The man chosen to blend the vision of a hockey arena and a convention center was C. Howard Crane. He was considered a master of architectural acoustics, so it is little wonder that Olympia Stadium would be known as a place where fan excitement was amplified. The building's seating sloped at such a steep angle that fans felt they were right on top of the action. At the time it was built, the Olympia was the largest indoor skating rink in the United States. Its 77,393 square feet of floor space concealed 74,880 square feet of pipes for the freezing of ice.

There was no single opening day for the Olympia. On October 15, 1927, an eight-day rodeo began, with ceremonies on October 17. Nine days later, fifteen thousand fans crammed into the new stadium to witness the first of many boxing matches.

The Red Wings called the Olympia home for more than fifty years before moving to Joe Louis Arena in 1979. (G.G. from Hoxie, Kansas, USA—Olympia arena (demolished) from HABSUploaded by Imzadi1979, License: CC BY 2.0; Source: https://commons.wikimedia.org/w/index.php?curid=11404691)

The NHL came to the Olympia on November 22, 1927, when the Cougars faced off against the Ottawa Senators. The ceremonies that took place that night incorporated professional figure skating between periods and performances by the University of Michigan marching band. Though the Senators spoiled the party by winning the game, 2–1, there was no question hockey was a hit in Detroit.

"Hockey, they discovered, is football set to lightning," the *Detroit Times* wrote of the reaction by fans. "The athletes flashed around the big expanse of ice like shooting stars, but every electric movement meant something. They squirmed, dodged, ducked, danced and pirouetted on their flashing blades with such rapidity that at times the eye could not quite follow the maneuvers. . . . That the pastime has caught on here cannot be doubted."

James Norris bought the Olympia and all of its interests in 1932 for $100,000, and the Red Wings brought the Stanley Cup to Detroit for the first time four years later, The Wings went on to win the Cup four times in six seasons from 1949–50 through 1954–55 and were a consistent playoff team through the late 1960s.

The Olympia's original seating capacity was 11,563. On June 23, 1965, work began to add 81 feet to the rear of the building. The addition included more seating and an escalator to improve fans' access to the upper levels. The seating capacity expanded to 13,375 in 1966, with standing room for 3,300 during hockey games. In 1970, private boxes were added.

The Wings declined in the late 1960s and into the 1970s, as did the neighborhood around the Olympia. When the NFL's Detroit Lions moved to suburban Pontiac, Michigan, in 1975, the Red Wings nearly followed. However, the city's offer of a riverfront arena kept the team in Detroit.

On December 15, 1979, the Red Wings played their final game at the Olympia, a 4–4 tie with the Quebec Nordiques. Detroit trailed, 4–1, after two periods but scored three times in the final 20 minutes to earn a point. Wings defenseman Greg Joly went down in history as the last player to score a goal at the Olympia when he tied the game at 18:35 of the third period.

34 The Stanley Cup Final was changed to a best-of-seven format in 1939. Since then, the Final has gone to a seventh game 16 times, but only two of those games had to go past regulation to determine a winner.

Those two games were played in 1950 and 1954, and the Red Wings were victorious each time.

In 1950, the Red Wings were expected to breeze past the New York Rangers in the Final. Not only had the Red Wings finished first in the regular season, 21 points ahead of the fourth-place Rangers, the Rangers would not have a home game, as a circus had priority over hockey at Madison Square Garden. As many as five games would be played at the Olympia, with Games 2 and 3 staged in Toronto with the Rangers as the "home" team. But someone forgot to tell the Rangers they were supposed to roll over for the mighty Wings.

Back-to-back overtime goals by Don Raleigh in Games 4 and 5 gave the Rangers a 3–2 series lead, and the Red Wings had to rally to even the series with a 5–4 win in Game 6.

The Rangers led, 2–0 and 3–2 in Game 7, only to have the Red Wings pull even, sending Game 7 of the Final into overtime for the first time.

Harry Lumley of the Wings and Chuck Rayner of the Rangers were perfect through the first overtime and well into the second. The Rangers nearly won it when Raleigh beat Lumley but drilled his shot off the crossbar.

The end then came suddenly. After George Gee won a draw, Pete Babando whipped a shot past Rayner at 8:31 of the second overtime, giving the Red Wings a 4–3 win and the Cup.

Four years later, the Red Wings and Montreal Canadiens found themselves at the Olympia getting ready for Game 7. The Wings had won three of the first four games, but Montreal had stayed alive with a 1–0 win at Detroit in Game 5 and a 4–1 victory at the Forum in Game 6.

Floyd Curry put Montreal ahead by beating Terry Sawchuk midway through the first period, but Red Kelly's power-play goal 1:17 into the second period got Detroit even. The rest of the second period and all of the third belonged to the goaltenders, Sawchuk and Montreal's Gerry McNeil.

The game headed into overtime tied, 1–1, but this time the Wings didn't need long to send their fans home happy. Forward Tony Leswick, who had played for the Rangers against Detroit in the 1950 Final but was now a Red Wing, was at the right point when Glen Skov's shot from the left wing missed the net and came all the way up to him, just inside the blue line. Leswick's harmless-looking wrist shot hit the glove of Montreal defenseman Doug Harvey and went past McNeil at 4:29 for the win, giving Detroit its third championship in five seasons.

35 Gordie Howe was a fixture at the NHL All-Star Game. From 1948, when he appeared for the first time, to 1980, when his final appearance nearly blew the roof off Joe Louis Arena, Howe appeared in a total of 23 All-Star Games, 22 as a member of the Red Wings. (He represented the Hartford Whalers in 1980, when he had returned to the NHL after six seasons in the World Hockey Association.)

Howe's first All-Star Game in 1948 is notable for the fact that he and Gus Mortson of the Stanley Cup champion Toronto Maple Leafs got into a fight and received five-minute majors, the first ones in All-Star history. He got his first All-Star goal and assist two years later, when the Red Wings, as defending champs, routed the All-Stars, 7–1.

Regardless the game's format, Howe was an All-Star Game regular through 1955. He wasn't chosen for the 1956 game, then held before the start of the regular season, but was chosen for every subsequent game through 1971, his last season with the Wings.

Howe's biggest offensive night as an All-Star was in 1965, when he scored two goals and had two assists to tie a record with four points. His first goal of the night stood as the game-winner in the All-Stars' 5–2 victory.

Howe's final All-Star Game scoring line is 10 goals, nine assists, and 19 points, along with 25 penalty minutes (an All-Star Game record that's likely to last for some time, given the scant number of penalties called today). All but an assist in the 1980 game came while he was a member of the Red Wings.

36 Steve Yzerman made No. 19 his own when he arrived in Detroit in 1983. But the reason he wanted to wear that number had nothing to do with the Red Wings and everything to do with his favorite player.

When Yzerman was a teenager in the early 1980s, playing for the Nepean Raiders and then the Peterborough Petes, he had plenty of hockey heroes to choose from. But his hero was New York Islanders center Bryan Trottier, one of the greatest two-way centers in NHL history and a cornerstone of the Islanders' dynasty in the early 1980s. Trottier wore No. 19, so that's the number Yzerman wanted as well.

Yzerman paid tribute to Trottier when he was inducted into the Hockey Hall of Fame in 2009, 12 years after his boyhood idol.

"The reason I chose No. 19, and I think the reason a lot of players chose 19 and played the way they did, was because of No. 19 of the New York Islanders, Bryan Trottier," Yzerman said. "I wore that number in his honor. He was a player I looked up to and admired."

Yzerman had good taste in heroes. Trottier won the Calder Trophy at age 19 in his rookie season, and the Art Ross Trophy as the NHL's top scorer in 1978–79, as well as the Hart Trophy as the MVP that season. He won the Conn Smythe Trophy as the playoff MVP in 1980 and played on four Cup-winning teams with the Islanders, then two more with the Pittsburgh Penguins in the early 1990s,

"I wore No. 19 because of Bryan Trottier," Yzerman said. "I liked the overall aspect of his game. I liked the way he conducted himself on the ice. He was a quiet guy. He played really hard. Just a good all-around, prototypical center man who could do everything."

37 For much of the late 1990s and early 2000s, a Red Wings-Avalanche matchup late in the Stanley Cup Playoffs was a rite of spring. The teams played in the Western Conference Final in 1996, 1997, and 2002, as well as in the conference semifinals in 1999 and 2000.

Overall, the Avalanche won three of the five series. But the Red Wings were 2–1 in the three meetings in the Western Conference Final, and their seven-game victory in 2002 was especially sweet.

By the time the Wings and Avs met in 2002, there was no

goaltender Detroit fans wanted to see their heroes beat more than Colorado's Patrick Roy, who had beaten them in three of the first four series and led the Avalanche to the Cup in 1996 and 2001. It looked like Roy and his teammates might make it four out of five, when Colorado's Peter Forsberg scored 6:24 into overtime to give the Avalanche a 2–1 win in Game 5 at Joe Louis Arena.

The Avalanche were leading the series 3–2 and would have a chance to eliminate the Wings back in Denver. But Dominik Hasek outplayed Roy in Game 6, and the Red Wings won 2–0 to even the series and send it back to Detroit for Game 7 (the first one between the teams in their five series).

Three of the first six games had been decided in overtime, one by a single goal and the others by two goals, so the fans who packed Joe Louis Arena on May 31, 2002, were expecting another tense, taut game. Instead, they got a laugher.

Tomas Holmstrom put the Red Wings in front to stay when he beat Roy on Detroit's first shot of the game, 1:57 after the opening faceoff. Sergei Fedorov made it 2–0 at 3:17 on Detroit's second shot, and Luc Robitaille beat Roy at 10:25, giving the Red Wings a 3–0 lead. Holmstrom scored again at 12:51, giving Detroit a 4–0 lead before the game was 13 minutes old.

Any dreams of a comeback the Avs might have had disappeared early in the second period, when Brett Hull scored at 4:41. Fredrik Olausson made it 6–0 at 6:28, and that was the end of the night for Roy, who was replaced by David Aebischer after surrendering six goals on 16 shots.

"I guess the tank was pretty close to being empty," Roy said after one of the worst playoff performances of his Hall of Fame career.

Pavel Datsyuk's third-period power-play goal capped a 7–0 win that sent Detroit into the Stanley Cup Final against the Carolina Hurricanes.

Even in their wildest dreams, the Wings hadn't expected that kind of game.

"We thought coming in, be prepared to go into overtime, or it would be a 1–0 game or 2–1 game," Steve Yzerman said. "After the

Pavel Datsyuk, aka "Magic Man," was a two-time Cup winner with the Red Wings. (Michael Righi—originally posted to Flickr as Pavel Datsyuk; License: CC BY-SA 2.0; Source: https://commons.wikimedia.org/w/index.php?curid=4185459)

first period, it's 4–0 and we're thinking, this isn't the way it's supposed to be. We're as surprised as anybody."

38 The Red Wings were among the NHL's elite teams throughout Mike Babcock's 10 seasons as coach. The New York Islanders were not. They qualified for the Stanley Cup playoffs just three times during that span and never won a playoff series. But for whatever reason, the Islanders owned the Wings during Babcock's time in Detroit.

The teams played 12 times during Babcock's decade in Detroit, and the Red Wings won just three of those games (twice in regulation, once in overtime).

The Islanders won, 2–1, at Detroit on December 4, 2005, the first of New York's five consecutive wins at Joe Louis Arena.

Perhaps the most unlikely of those victories came on March 27, 2009, when former Red Wings backup goaltender Joey MacDonald made 42 saves in a 2–0 victory. The Islanders scored twice in the second period, and the Wings spent the rest of the night bombing away at MacDonald without success. Detroit went 0-for-6 on the power play against the Islanders, who finished the season with the NHL's worst record.

The Islanders also spoiled New Year's Eve in 2013 with a 4–3 overtime victory. In all, New York outscored Detroit, 38–27, shut out the Red Wings three times, and limited them to one goal in three other games.

39 The Red Wings and octopus-throwing have become synonymous. It wouldn't be playoff time in Detroit without an octopus or two (or three, or four) hitting the ice.

The concept of the octopus dates to the Original Six era, when there were just two rounds of the Stanley Cup Playoffs and a team needed eight wins to take home a championship.

Legend has it that the custom of chucking cephalopods in the postseason was the creation of the Cusimano brothers, Pete and Jerry. Owners of a local fish market in Detroit, the pair believed that the octopus made for a natural good luck charm, because its eight tentacles symbolized the number of wins needed to secure the Stanley Cup in the Original Six era.

As Pete Cusimano told the *Detroit Free Press* years later, he remembers Jerry saying, "Here's the thing with eight legs. Why don't we throw it on the ice and maybe the Wings will win eight straight?"

The first octopus hit the ice on April 15, 1952, when the Red Wings played the Montreal Canadiens at the Olympia in Game 4 of the Stanley Cup Final after winning the first three games of the series. After Gordie Howe scored the game's first goal, Pete hopped out of his seat and hurled his stowaway octopus onto the ice. The Red Wings went on to complete the sweep and take home the Cup.

The rest is history. The octopus has become the symbol of playoff hockey in Detroit, even though today's teams need 16 wins to capture the Cup.

40 Ever do something you wish you could undo? Detroit general manager Jack Adams probably had that feeling in the summer of 1957.

Two years earlier, Adams had traded goaltender Terry Sawchuk, who was coming off a five-year stretch that had been as good as any in NHL history, because he had a hot young (and less costly) goaltender named Glenn Hall ready to take the starting job.

With Hall ready, Adams felt he could trade Sawchuk without harming the future of a team that had won its fourth Stanley Cup in a span of six seasons.

The GM engineered a nine-player trade with the Boston Bruins. Sawchuk was the biggest name—by far. The Red Wings got a package of five young players, though only stay-at-home defenseman Warren Godfrey remained in Detroit for any significant length of time (seven seasons).

Hall was superb during the next two seasons, playing every minute of every game. But the Red Wings, who had won the Cup in 1954 and 1955, lost to the Montreal Canadiens in the Final in 1956, then were upset by the Bruins in the 1957 Semifinals.

Adams realized that getting rid of Sawchuk hadn't worked out and decided to get him back. On July 10, 1957, the Bruins sent Sawchuk back to Detroit in a trade for left wing Johnny Bucyk and cash. Hall was sent to the lowly Chicago Black Hawks less than two weeks later, along with Wings captain Ted Lindsay. Adams had been furious at Lindsay's efforts to organize a players union, and the Hawks were regarded as the NHL's version of Siberia at the time (though that was soon to change).

Unfortunately for the Red Wings, Sawchuk was solid in his return, but was no longer the all-star he had been in his first go-around with the team. Even worse was the fact that Bucyk, who had scored 10 goals and had 21 points in 66 games during 1956–57 while trying to break into a lineup filled with stars, soon became one of the NHL's most reliable scorers in Boston. He had 21 goals and 52 points in his first season with the Bruins and went on to score 545 of his 556 NHL goals in black and gold, earning a berth in the Hockey Hall of Fame.

THIRD PERIOD

A few minutes of rest, a chance to dry out the gloves, and a few words of wisdom from the coaching staff. OK, it's crunch time, and we're off to the third period.

1 The Red Wings hold the NHL regular-season record with 62 wins. When did they set the record? *Answer on page 145.*
   a. 1993–94
   b. 1994–95
   c. 1995–96
   d. 1996–97

2 Defenseman Kyle Quincey, who spent eight seasons with the Wings between 2005 and 2016, was the second of only two players whose last name begins with "Q" to wear the winged wheel. Who was the first? *Answer on page 146.*

3 The Red Wings selected Steve Yzerman with the fourth pick in the 1983 NHL Draft, but they also had good success in the lower rounds. How many players taken by the Red Wings that year went on to play at least 700 games in the NHL? *Answer on page 147.*
   a. 3
   b. 4
   c. 5
   d. 6

4 Gordie Howe played more games for the Red Wings than anyone else, but one franchise record he doesn't hold is for most penalty minutes in a career. Who is the most penalized player in Red Wings history? *Answer on page 149.*
   a. Joe Kocur
   b. Ted Lindsay
   c. Bob Probert
   d. Howie Young

5 "Smith" is the most common surname in Red Wings history. How many players who've played for Detroit since the franchise entered the NHL in 1926 have been named Smith? *Answer on page 150.*
   a. 12
   b. 14
   c. 16
   d. 18

6 Normie Smith is one of two Red Wings goaltenders who had a shutout in his first Stanley Cup Playoff game. The other one had a much easier time. Who was he? *Answer on page 151.*
   a. Roger Crozier
   b. Dominik Hasek
   c. Ed Mio
   d. Chris Osgood

7 The Red Wings have had the No. 1 selection in the NHL draft once in the past 40 years. What year did they have that first pick and which player did they select? *Answers on page 153.*

8 Four players have accounted for the five seasons in which a Red Wing accumulated 300 or more penalty minutes. Who is the only player to do it twice? *Answer on page 154.*

a. Joe Kocur
b. Dennis Polonich
c. Bob Probert
d. Bryan Watson

9 Only one member of the Red Wings has ever had a rating of plus-50 or better in a single season. Who accomplished that feat? *Answer on page 155.*
a. Sergei Fedorov
b. Vladimir Konstantinov
c. Nicklas Lidstrom
d. Steve Yzerman

10 Steve Yzerman set a Red Wings record for points in a season when he had 155 in 1988–89. Whose team mark did he break? *Answer on page 156.*
a. Marcel Dionne
b. Sergei Fedorov
c. Gordie Howe
d. John Ogrodnick

11 It wasn't the case during the time he played in the NHL, but the Gordie Howe Hat Trick—a goal, an assist, and a fighting major in the same game—has become a recognized fan-made statistic. (The NHL does not officially track this stat.) How many GHHTs did Howe actually have? *Answer on page 157.*
a. 0
b. 2
c. 4
d. 6

12 In 1999–2000, the Red Wings had one hat trick during the regular season and one during the Stanley Cup Playoffs. The same player scored three goals in each game. Who was he? *Answer on page 158.*

    a. Kris Draper
    b. Sergei Fedorov
    c. Martin Lapointe
    d. Brendan Shanahan

13 The same Red Wings player took the first eight penalty shots in franchise history, from November 15, 1934, through December 29, 1935. Who was he? *Answer on page 159.*
    a. Larry Aurie
    b. Charlie Conacher
    c. Ebbie Goodfellow
    d. John Sorrell

14 Gordie Howe won the Art Ross Trophy as the NHL's top scorer six times. Who is the only other Red Wing to win the award? *Answer on page 160.*
    a. Alex Delvecchio
    b. Ted Lindsay
    c. Frank Mahovlich
    d. Steve Yzerman

15 The Red Wings have had at least one hat trick in every season except three since the NHL's Expansion Era began in 1967. In which seasons did no Red Wing score three goals in a game? *Answer on page 161.*

16 Gordie Howe retired in 1971. Who is the only right wing to play for the Red Wings and make a postseason All-Star team since then? *Answer on page 161.*
    a. Mike Foligno
    b. Johan Franzen
    c. Johan Garpenlov
    d. Mickey Redmond

17 Nine goaltenders have won 100 or more games with Detroit. Only one of them had more losses than wins. Who is he? *Answer on page 162.*
   a. Tim Cheveldae
   b. Manny Legace
   c. Eddie Mio
   d. Greg Stefan

18 The Lady Byng Trophy is given by the NHL to recognize the player who best combines skillful and gentlemanly play. One member of the Red Wings has won it four times. Who is he? *Answer on page 164.*

19 Five Red Wings have hit double figures in game-winning goals in a single season, but only one has had more than 10— and he did it twice. Who is the most prolific single-season generator of game-winning goals? *Answer on page 165.*
   a. Sergei Fedorov
   b. Brendan Shanahan
   c. Ray Sheppard
   d. Paul Ysebaert

20 Only one member of the Red Wings has averaged more than 26 minutes of ice time per game for a full season since the NHL made time on ice an official statistic in the 1990s— and he did it 10 times. Who is this iron man? *Answer on page 166.*
   a. Chris Chelios
   b. Niklas Kronwall
   c. Nicklas Lidstrom
   d. Larry Murphy

21 Eight players share the Red Wings' career record for over-time goals in the Stanley Cup Playoffs with two. How many of them did it in the same playoff year? *Answer on page 167.*

a. 0
b. 1
c. 2
d. 3

22 Gordie Howe is still the Red Wings' all-time leader in points during the regular season. But who holds the team record for career points in the Stanley Cup Playoffs? *Answer on page 168.*

a. Sergei Fedorov
b. Gordie Howe
c. Nicklas Lidstrom
d. Steve Yzerman

23 The Red Wings played 815 ties before the NHL adopted the shootout in 2005 to decide games that remained deadlocked after a five-minute overtime period. Of all the other franchises that were active from 1926 to 2017, which one never played a game against the Red Wings that ended in a tie? Which one played the most ties against the Wings? *Answers on page 169.*

24 Goaltenders aren't known for their offensive contributions, but they'll pick up a few points here and there. Which goaltender is the all-time points leader for the Red Wings? *Answer on page 170.*

a. Tim Cheveldae
b. Chris Osgood
c. Greg Stefan
d. Terry Sawchuk

25 Goaltender Dave Gagnon's career with the Red Wings lasted all of two games during the 1990–91 season. But he earned a line in the NHL history books because of a goal he allowed to a future Red Wing on January 25, 1991. Why was that goal one for the record books? *Answer on page 171.*

26 The Red Wings' record for shutouts by a goaltender in one season is 12, and it's held by two Hockey Hall of Famers. Terry Sawchuk did it three times in the early 1950s. Who is the other Detroit goaltender to have a dozen shutouts in one season? *Answer on page 172.*
a. Glenn Hall
b. Dominik Hasek
c. Hap Holmes
d. John Ross Roach

27 The Wings were one of the most successful teams in the NHL during the Original Six era (1942 to 1967). They finished first in the regular-season standings 10 times and won the Stanley Cup five times. They finished last in the six-team league just once. When did it happen? *Answer on page 173.*
a. 1945–46
b. 1955–56
c. 1958–59
d. 1966–67

28 The Red Wings won the Stanley Cup four times from 1997 to 2008. In how many of those seasons did they finish first in their division? *Answer on page 175.*
a. 0
b. 1
c. 2
d. 3

29 New Year's Eve is a hockey holiday in Detroit, one in which the Red Wings almost always play at home. After defeating the Pittsburgh Penguins, 4–1, on December 31, 2017, the Wings were 36–24–8–1. They've played four overtime games on December 31 and are 2–2, with the two losses coming against the same team. Which team was it? *Answer on page 176.*

a. Boston Bruins

b. Chicago Blackhawks

c. Montreal Canadiens

d. New York Islanders

30 Ten men have served as general manager of the Red Wings (technically, Jim Devellano has done it twice). How many were Hall of Fame players for the Red Wings before moving into the GM's chair? *Answer on page 177.*

a. 2

b. 3

c. 4

d. 5

31 Coach Mike Babcock wore a "lucky" tie during the 2008 Stanley Cup Playoffs. What university did it honor? *Answer on page 178.*

a. Alabama-Huntsville

b. McGill

c. Michigan State

d. Northern Michigan

32 The Carlson brothers remain cult figures to a lot of hockey fans, because of their fictional Hanson brothers characters in the 1977 movie "Slap Shot." Steve and Jeff Carlson played the Steve and Jeff Hanson characters, while their cinematic brother, Jack Hanson, was portrayed by David Hanson. All were hockey players in real life. Which of them actually played for the Wings? *Answer on page 179.*

33 Among his many distinctions, Gordie Howe shares one with Mario Lemieux and Guy Lafleur. What did those three players accomplish that no one else has? *Answer on page 180.*

a. Played in the NHL after being inducted into the Hockey Hall of Fame

b. Played in the NHL after turning 45

c. Scored 70 goals in a season

d. Won the Stanley Cup in four consecutive seasons

34 The Jack Adams Award is given annually to the NHL's coach of the year. But when Adams was actually coaching the Red Wings, the league named First-Team and Second-Team All-Star coaches. How many times was Adams selected as First-Team coach, the equivalent of today's trophy? *Answer on page 181.*

a. 0

b. 1

c. 2

d. 3

35 The Kharlamov Trophy was instituted in 2002 and originally given each season to the best Russian player in the NHL. It's now awarded to the best Russian player in the NHL and the Kontinental Hockey League. Two Red Wings have won the trophy, which is named in honor of Valeri Kharlamov, a longtime star in the Soviet Union. Who are they? *Answer on page 183.*

36 How many Red Wings named Howe are members of the Hockey Hall of Fame? *Answer on page 184.*

a. 1

b. 2

c. 3

d. 4

37 Gordie Howe won the Hart Trophy, given to the NHL's most valuable player, six times, but he was not the first member of the Red Wings to win it. Who was? *Answer on page 186.*
a. Sid Abel
b. Ebbie Goodfellow
c. Syd Howe
d. Carl Voss

38 The Red Wings entered the NHL as the Detroit Cougars. They had one other nickname before becoming known by their current name in 1932. What was it? *Answer on page 187.*
a. Bengals
b. Falcons
c. Tigers
d. Wolverines

39 Terry Sawchuk staged one of the greatest goaltending exhibitions in hockey history while helping the Red Wings win the Stanley Cup in 1952. How many goals did Sawchuk allow during Detroit's back-to-back sweeps? There's a bonus point if you know the home-road split. *Answers on page 187.*
a. 5
b. 7
c. 9
d. 11

40 The Red Wings have had players born in a number of countries, but only one who can list Beirut, Lebanon, as his birthplace. He's also the only NHL player born there. Who is he? *Answer on page 189.*

THIRD PERIOD—
ANSWERS

1 By the early 1990s, the Red Wings' rebuilding efforts under Jim Devellano and his management team were beginning to bear fruit. Longtime star Steve Yzerman, who had put up huge scoring numbers with less than stellar teams in the 1980s, was learning to sacrifice some of his offense to play better two-way hockey. Nicklas Lidstrom was emerging as one of the NHL's best defensemen, and the nucleus of the team that would end Detroit's Stanley Cup drought was coming together.

With the NHL having realigned into Eastern and Western conferences and four divisions for the 1993–94 season, the Red Wings overcame the loss of Yzerman for most of the season and rolled to a first-place finish in the Central Division with a 46–30–8 record and 100 points.

It looked like they'd gotten an easy opponent in the opening round of the Stanley Cup Playoffs, when the third-year San Jose Sharks earned the final postseason spot from the Western Conference. But someone forgot to tell the Sharks they were supposed to be intimidated. San Jose won the series opener at Joe Louis Arena, fought the Wings to a stalemate through six games, then stunned the packed house at the Joe with a 4–3 victory in Game 7.

Had the 1994–95 season not been reduced to 48 games by a lockout, the Red Wings might have set an NHL record for wins. As it was, they led the NHL with a 33–11–4 record and 70 points. There was lots of optimism that this would be the year the Cup drought, now 40 years old, would come to an end.

Detroit went 12–2 in defeating the Dallas Stars, the Sharks, and the Chicago Blackhawks to win the Western Conference championship.

But despite having the home-ice advantage in the Final, the Red Wings were swept by the New Jersey Devils.

The Red Wings showed no aftereffects from their failure in the Final when they took the ice for the 1995–96 season. With Scotty Bowman orchestrating from behind the bench, the Wings won an NHL-record 62 games (two more than the Bowman-coached 1976–77 Montreal Canadiens) and won the Presidents' Trophy with 131 points (62–13–7). At a minimum, they were expected to get back to the Stanley Cup Final, but, after defeating the pesky Winnipeg Jets in six games and outlasting the St. Louis Blues in seven, the Wings couldn't get past the Colorado Avalanche in the Western Conference Final. The Avs, playing their first season in Denver after relocating from Quebec, won the series in six games before sweeping the Florida Panthers in the Final.

Ironically, the Red Wings won the Cup the following season—after a regular season in which they dropped to second place and fell to 94 points (36–28–18) after their 62-win, 131-point season in 1995–96.

2 Defenseman Kyle Quincey has had two stints with the Red Wings. He played a total of 13 games in three seasons from 2005–06 through 2007–08, then rejoined the Wings late in the 2011–12 season and played with Detroit through 2015–16.

Before Quincey joined the Wings, they'd had exactly one other player in franchise history whose last name began with the letter "Q"—and, like Quincey, he was a defenseman.

Bill Quackenbush caught the attention of the Red Wings by putting up 34 points in 23 games for the Brantford Lions of the Ontario Hockey Association in 1941–42. The Red Wings signed him as a free agent, and by the end of the following season, he had already made his NHL debut with the Wings, putting up a goal and an assist in 10 games.

Quackenbush became a full-time NHL player in 1943–44, finishing with four goals and 18 points in 43 games. For the next five seasons, he was a regular on Detroit's blue line, though he relied on his skating and puckhandling skills rather than playing a physical game.

Quackenbush was voted a Second-Team All-Star in 1946–47, when he had five goals, 22 points, and six penalty minutes. He again had 22 points (six goals, 16 assists) in 1947–48, and this time was voted a First-Team All-Star.

He repeated his First-Team All-Star appearance in 1948–49, finishing with 23 points (six goals, 17 assists) without taking a penalty in 60 games. And this time Quackenbush took home an award, as well: He won the Lady Byng Trophy in recognition of his skill and sportsmanship, becoming the first defenseman, one of just three in NHL history, to take home the trophy.

That trophy also earned Quackenbush a ticket out of town. Wings GM Jack Adams wasn't a fan of the Lady Byng and felt that a player who won it didn't belong on his team. Despite being a First-Team All-Star in back-to-back seasons, Quackenbush was traded to the Boston Bruins on August 16, 1949. He played seven seasons with the Bruins before retiring after the 1955–56 season and was inducted into the Hockey Hall of Fame in 1976.

3 When Detroit fans think of the 1983 NHL Draft, the first name that comes to mind is Steve Yzerman.

That's because the Red Wings were fortunate enough to select Yzerman with the fourth pick in the 1983 draft. After the Minnesota North Stars took Brian Lawton with the first pick and the Hartford Whalers selected Sylvain Turgeon No. 2, the New York Islanders disappointed a lot of Detroit fans (and GM Jim Devellano) by taking local favorite Pat LaFontaine with the third pick.

Yzerman, then a pimply-faced 18 year old, was taken by the Red Wings with the fourth pick. He spent his entire career with the Wings, played more than 1,500 games, and was a first-ballot selection to the Hockey Hall of Fame.

Nabbing a player like Yzerman would make any draft a success. But Devellano and his scouting staff also found three other players who played more than 700 NHL games and made an impact with the Wings.

The Red Wings hit it big with their third-round pick. Bob Probert, a big, tough forward with some scoring touch, was taken by Detroit in the third round (No. 46). He joined the Red Wings in 1985–86 and became the NHL's most feared heavyweight. But Probert could do a lot more than fight. He had 29 goals and 62 points (and 398 penalty minutes) in 1987–88 and 13 or more goals in his first five full seasons with Detroit.

Probert left the Red Wings and signed with the Chicago Black-hawks as a free agent in the summer of 1994. He finished his career after the 2001–02 season with 163 goals, 384 points, and 3,300 penalty minutes in 935 NHL games.

The Wings came up winners again in the fifth round with a different kind of forward. Petr Klima, a native of Czechoslovakia, was taken (No. 86). Klima joined the Red Wings in 1985–86 and was an instant hit, scoring 32 goals in his first NHL season. He had 30 and 37 goals in his next two seasons, and 25 goals in 51 games in 1988–89.

But on November 2, 1989, the Red Wings sent Klima to the Edmonton Oilers as part of a blockbuster trade that brought high-scoring, Detroit-area native Jimmy Carson to the Wings. Klima had 25 of his 30 goals in 1989–90 with the Oilers and scored at 15:13 of the third overtime in Game 1 of the 1990 Stanley Cup Final, helping the Oilers win their fifth championship in seven seasons. Klima also played for the Los Angeles Kings, Pittsburgh Penguins, Tampa Bay Lightning, and the Oilers again before finishing his career with the Wings in 1998–99. He ended his NHL career with 313 goals and 573 points in 786 games. He had the first five of his nine hat tricks while playing for Detroit.

Two picks after selecting Klima, the Red Wings had another success when they took Joe Kocur, a big, tough wing from Saskatoon of the Western Hockey League. Kocur and Probert gave the Wings the most physical pair of forwards in the NHL. Kocur led the NHL with 377 penalty minutes in 1985–86 and had 200 or more PIM in each of his first six seasons with the Wings before being traded to the New York Rangers on March 5, 1991.

Kocur was part of the Rangers' 1994 Stanley Cup-winning team, then helped the Wings win it all in 1997 and 1998. He retired after the 1998–99 season with 80 goals, 162 points, and 2,519 penalty minutes in 820 games.

The Wings made it a troika of tough guys when they chose Stu Grimson in the 10th round (No. 186). They didn't sign Grimson, who went back into the draft and was taken by the Calgary Flames two years later in the seventh round (No. 143), but he played 68 games for the Wings from 1994–96. Grimson ended up playing for seven NHL teams, finishing with 17 goals, 39 points, and 2,113 penalty minutes in 729 games.

4 Gordie Howe piled up 1,643 penalty minutes in 1,687 games during his 25 seasons with the Red Wings and retired as the most penalized player in team history, as well as the Wings' all-time leader in goals and points, in 1971.

But records are made to be broken, so the old cliché goes, and Howe's career mark for penalty minutes is no exception.

Though he's been gone from the Wings for more than 40 years, Howe's total is still good for third in franchise history. The only players he trails were teammates in the 1980s and early 1990s selected two rounds apart in the 1983 NHL Draft.

Fifth-round pick Joe Kocur, a big, tough forward from Western Canada, racked up 377 penalty minutes as a rookie in 1985–86. That number dropped as he became known as one of the most feared fighters in the NHL, but he still piled up more than 200 minutes in each of his six seasons with Detroit before being dealt to the New York Rangers at the 1991 NHL trade deadline.

Kocur returned to the Red Wings in 1996 and spent his final three seasons with Detroit, serving as a physical presence on the "Grind Line" for much of that time and playing on back-to-back Cup-winning teams in 1997 and '98. He totaled 249 penalty minutes in those three seasons, giving him 1,963 in 535 games with Detroit.

That's 320 more than Howe, but 127 less than the Red Wings' all-time leader, Bob Probert.

Probert came to the Wings along with Kocur, in 1985–86. He was a better offensive contributor than Kocur, finishing with eight goals and 21 points in 44 games, along with 186 penalty minutes.

Probert had 221 penalty minutes in 1986–87, while putting up 13 goals and 24 points in 63 games, then had one of the most remarkable seasons in NHL history in 1987–88. He made his lone appearance in the NHL All-Star Game and finished with 29 goals and 62 points—all while leading the league in penalty minutes with 398, setting a Red Wings single-season record in the process. For good measure, he scored eight goals and had 21 points—and 51 penalty minutes—in 16 playoff games.

After missing all but 29 games during the next two seasons, Probert played at least 55 games in each of the next four seasons. He scored 57 goals during that span while taking at least 275 penalty minutes in each season.

Probert signed with the Chicago Blackhawks in the summer of 1994 and spent the rest of his NHL career in the Windy City. He left Detroit having taken a team-record 2,090 penalty minutes in just 474 games.

5 From Alex in 1931–32 to Brendan in 2016–17, the Red Wings have had exactly 12 Smiths play for them since entering the NHL in 1926.

Alex Smith, a defenseman, joined the Detroit Falcons for the 1931–32 season after spending his first seven NHL seasons with the Ottawa Senators. He had six goals and 14 points in 48 games during his one season with Detroit, then returned to the Senators, then played for the Boston Bruins and New York Americans before retiring from the NHL in 1935.

The first of the two Smiths to play goal, Normie, joined the Red Wings in 1934–35, going 12–12–2 with a 2.01 goals-against average. He played every game in each of the next two seasons, leading the NHL in wins in 1935–36 (24) and 1936–37 (25). More important, he led the Red Wings to the Stanley Cup in each of those seasons. He was also the winning goaltender in the longest NHL game ever played, a six-overtime 1–0 win against the Montreal Maroons in Game 1 of the 1936 Semifinals.

Normie Smith didn't last much longer in Detroit. After injuring his arm and going 11–25–11 in 1937–38, he didn't show up for a game early in the 1938–39 season. An angry GM Jack Adams traded him to the Boston Bruins. But Smith refused to report and retired, though he did rejoin the Red Wings briefly in 1943–44 and 1944–45, when World War II left NHL teams short of talent.

There were actually three Smiths who played for the Red Wings in 1943–44, when brothers Carl and Dalton "Nakina" Smith, both forwards, spent their only seasons in Detroit.

The next Smith to join the Red Wings was Brian, a forward who played 61 games with Detroit during three seasons from 1957–58 through 1960–61. Floyd Smith, a center, joined the Red Wings in 1962–63 and spent nearly six full seasons in Detroit, contributing 93 goals and 215 points in 347 games before being traded to the Toronto Maple Leafs on March 3, 1968.

Goaltender Al Smith was claimed by the Red Wings from the Pittsburgh Penguins in the 1971 NHL waiver draft and played 43 games during his lone season with Detroit, going 18–20–4 with a 3.24 goals-against average. He signed with the New England Whalers of the World Hockey Association for the 1972–73 season.

The 1980s were a boom time for Smiths in Detroit. Forwards Brad Smith (1980–81 to 1984–85) and Derek Smith (1981–82 to 1982–83), as well as defensemen Greg Smith (1981–82 to 1985–86) and Rick Smith (1980–81) all spent time with the Red Wings.

The Red Wings then went nearly two decades without a Smith until Brendan, a defenseman who was their first-round pick (No. 27) in the 2007 NHL Draft, made it to the NHL in 2011–12. He played 291 games with Detroit until being traded to the Rangers on February 28, 2017.

6 Normie Smith's six-OT, 1–0 victory against the Montreal Maroons in Game 1 of the 1936 Semifinals came in his first Stanley Cup Playoff game with the Red Wings. To say that the only other Red Wings goaltender to put up a shutout in his first postseason game with Detroit had an easier time would be putting it mildly.

Chris Osgood was a 21-year-old rookie in 1993–94 who earned a chance to play in the postseason after going 23–8–5 during the regular season. He sat for the Red Wings' playoff opener against the San Jose Sharks and saw the third-year team score five times against veteran Bob Essensa in a stunning 5–4 win at Joe Louis Arena.

Coach Scotty Bowman made a change in Game 2, opting to let Osgood make his playoff debut against the Sharks on April 20, 1994.

Ozzie's teammates made it easy for him, allowing the Sharks just 22 shots on goal, and Osgood stopped them all on the way to a 4–0 victory. Shawn Burr gave the Wings a 1–0 lead 47 seconds into the second period, and third-period goals by Bob Probert, Dino Ciccarelli, and Nicklas Lidstrom put the game away.

Chris Osgood is one of two Red Wings goaltenders to have a shutout in his first Stanley Cup Playoff game. (Michael Miller—Own work, License: CC BY-SA 3.0, Source: https://commons.wikimedia.org/w/index.php?curid=18302447)

Osgood started each of the five remaining games in the series. He got the win in Game 3, took the loss in a 4–3 defeat in Game 4, and was pulled early in the first period of a 6–4 loss in Game 5. He and the Red Wings bounced back with a 7–1 win on the road in Game 6, but Osgood was the losing goaltender in San Jose's shocking 3–2 win in Game 7. .

7 From 1978 to the present, the Red Wings have had the No. 1 pick in the NHL Draft exactly once. (They did have the No. 1 pick in the 1964 Amateur Draft, selecting forward Claude Gauthier, who never played in the NHL, and took center Dale McCourt with the first pick in the 1977 draft.) Since then, the only time the Red Wings had the No. 1 selection in the draft was 1986.

They stayed local for that pick, choosing Michigan State forward Joe Murphy. The native of London, Ontario, was coming off a tremendous season for the Spartans in 1985–86, finishing with 24 goals and 61 points in 35 games. The Red Wings made him the first NCAA player to be taken No. 1 in the draft.

However, there was a problem. Murphy excelled as a center in college, but the Red Wings already had Steve Yzerman as their No. 1 center and Adam Oates in the middle on the second line. Murphy spent most of 1986–87, his first pro season, with Adirondack of the American Hockey League, putting up 21 goals and 59 points in 71 games. He had one assist in five games with Detroit.

Murphy had five goals and 11 points in six games with Adirondack in 1987–88, but spent most of the season with Detroit, scoring 10 goals and finishing with 19 points. However, he was back in Adirondack for most of 1988–89 and lit up the AHL, scoring 31 goals and piling up 66 points in 47 games before helping Adirondack win the Calder Cup.

By then, Murphy was a right wing, one who looked like he was ready to do big things in Detroit. Instead, his time with the Red Wings was almost up. After Murphy scored three goals in Detroit's first nine games in 1989–90, he was included in a package that brought back high-scoring Detroit-area native Jimmy Carson.

The trade worked out well for Murphy in the short run. He had seven goals and 25 points in 62 games with Edmonton, then helped the Oilers win their fifth Stanley Cup in seven seasons. He went on to play a total of 779 games in the NHL, retiring after playing 14 games for the Washington Capitals in 2000–01. He had two 30-goal seasons and five others in which he scored at least 20 goals, finishing his career with 233 goals and 528 points.

8 The two-decade span from 1974 to 1994 in the NHL was marked by big offensive numbers and huge amounts of penalty minutes being assessed. The success of the "Big Bad Bruins" and Philadelphia's "Broad Street Bullies" led other teams to make sure they had plenty of muscle. Fighting majors were plentiful, and misconduct penalties were handled out like parking tickets.

Defenseman Howie Young had set an NHL record with 273 penalty minutes in 1962–63, a mark that, at the time, looked like it could stand forever. But in 1975–76, two Red Wings not only had more penalty minutes than Young, they became the first Wings to exceed 300 minutes in a season.

Detroit defenseman Bryan Watson didn't score a goal, but he piled up 322 penalty minutes. Forward Dennis Polonich had 11 goals and 23 points in 57 games, piling up 302 PIM along the way.

Watson and Polonich were the only two Wings to exceed 300 penalty minutes in a season until the mid-1980s, when 1983 draft picks Joe Kocur and Bob Probert earned full-time positions and began taking penalty minutes by the boatload.

Kocur shattered Watson's single-season team record in 1985–86 by taking 377 penalty minutes—and amazingly, he needed just 59 games to do it, meaning that he averaged more than six penalty minutes per game. But that record didn't last long. In 1987–88, Probert piled up a team-record 398 penalty minutes in 74 games (though his per-game average was less than Kocur's). But while Kocur hadn't contributed much offensively while piling up his 377 penalty minutes, Probert found time between penalties to have his best offensive season, finishing with 29 goals and 62 points to earn a trip to the NHL All-Star Game.

No other member of the Red Wings reached 300 penalty minutes again until Probert had 315 in 55 games during the 1989–90 season, when he also contributed 16 goals and 39 points. No Detroit player has exceeded 300 minutes since then. In fact, the most by any Red Wings player since 2000 stands at 138, taken by Darren McCarty in 2002–03.

9 We'll never know what kind of plus/minus numbers the great Detroit teams of the Original Six era would have had. Even with the NHL's incredible effort to computerize its entire game-by-game history, plus/minus numbers don't exist before the 1959–60 season. Gordie Howe was plus-45 in 1968–69, when the Wings finished fifth and missed the Stanley Cup Playoffs. Picture what his numbers might have been when the Red Wings were winning four Cups in the six seasons from 1949 to 1955.

Since plus/minus became a recognized statistic, the Red Wings have had 18 seasons in which one of their players has finished at plus-40 or better. Nicklas Lidstrom had four of them, with a career-best plus-43 in 1993–94.

Four Red Wings—Howe, linemates Alex Delvecchio and Frank Mahovlich, and defenseman Gary Bergman—were all plus-40 or better in 1968–69, when Detroit finished fifth in the East Division with a 33–31–12 record. (They would have been second in the West, which was comprised of the six teams that entered the league in the 1967 expansion.) That team was dynamite at even strength but scored just 40 power-play goals and surrendered 61.

Forward Paul Ysebaert led the NHL in plus/minus in 1991–92 at plus-44. Detroit defensemen Brad McCrimmon (plus-39) and Lidstrom (plus-36) were second and third. Sergei Fedorov was plus-48 and plus-49 in back-to-back full seasons (1993–94 and 1995–96).

The 1994–95 season was reduced to 48 games by a lockout, but then Vladimir Konstantinov finished the 1995–96 season with a plus-60 rating, the best in the NHL by a considerable margin. (Fedorov's plus-49 was a distant second, and Detroit defenseman Viacheslav Fetisov was tied for third at plus-37.) And yet the only Detroit player to finish better than plus-50 in a season was a defenseman who wasn't a big scorer.

Konstantinov had joined the Red Wings in 1991–92 and was plus-22 or better in each of his first three NHL seasons, then plus-10 in the lockout-shortened 1994–95 season. But in 1995–96, when the Red Wings finished with a team-record 131 points, Konstantinov had an NHL career-high 14 goals and matched his NHL best with 34 points, in addition to leading the NHL in plus-minus.

Konstantinov was "only" plus-38 the following season, but he had a career-best 38 points and finished second in balloting for the Norris Trophy, helping the Red Wings to their first Stanley Cup championship since 1955. Unfortunately, his hockey career came to a tragic end on June 13, 1997, when the limousine he was riding in crashed into a tree. He was in a coma for several weeks, and sustained head injuries and paralysis that ended his hockey career.

10 Given the way the NHL is structured today, Steve Yzerman's 155 points in 1988–89 seem almost unreal. Yzerman's career year has never been challenged, and he owns the second- and third-highest single-season point totals in team history as well, raking in 137 in 1992–93 and 127 in 1989–90. (Can you imagine having 127 points in a season and having that be a 28-point drop from the previous season?)

Gordie Howe was the first member of the Red Wings to break the 100-point mark. Incredible as it may seem, he had 103 points in 1968–69, the season in which he turned 41. Howe's mark stood until 1974–75, when Marcel Dionne blew it away.

Dionne, taken by Detroit with the No. 2 pick in the 1971 NHL Draft, lit up the scoreboard as soon as he reached the NHL. He had 28 goals and 77 points as a rookie, put up 90 and 78 points in his next two seasons, then hit his stride in 1974–75.

Though the Red Wings missed the Stanley Cup Playoffs, Dionne had a spectacular season, finishing with 47 goals and a team-record 121 points. He had more power-play goals (15), than penalty minutes (14). The 121 points shattered Howe's team record, ranked him third in the NHL behind Bobby Orr (135) and Phil Esposito (127), and put him two points ahead of Montreal's Guy Lafleur, who was picked ahead of Dionne in the 1971 draft.

Dionne went on to have seven more seasons of 100-plus points, but none of them came with the Red Wings. He and team management couldn't agree on a new contract, and Dionne wound up joining the Los Angeles Kings, for whom he had his biggest seasons on the way to earning induction into the Hockey Hall of Fame in 1992.

11 The concept of the Gordie Howe Hat Trick—a goal, an assist, and a fighting major in the same game—didn't exist during Mr. Hockey's celebrated career. It was named after Howe because of his unique blend of hockey skill and toughness.

What's regarded today as the first Gordie Howe Hat Trick took place on December 22, 1920, when Harry Cameron, also a member of the Hockey Hall of Fame, had one for the Toronto St. Patricks (now the Toronto Maple Leafs).

According to the Society for International Hockey Research, the all-time leader in Gordie Howe Hat Tricks is Rick Tocchet, now coach of the Arizona Coyotes. Tocchet had 18 games (regular season and playoffs) in which he scored a goal, had an assist, and got into a fight. That's one more than runners-up Brendan Shanahan and Brian Sutter. Wilf Paiement is next with 16, followed by Jarome Iginla with 11.

Three players had Gordie Howe Hat Tricks when the Minnesota North Stars played the Boston Bruins on April 9, 1981. Minnesota's Bryan Maxwell and Bobby Smith each had Gordie Howe Hat Tricks for Minnesota, while Boston defenseman Brad Park scored a goal, had three assists, and fought Smith.

Tocchet had three Gordie Howe Hat Tricks during the 1986–87 season, one more than the man for whom it was named had during his 26 NHL seasons. Both of No. 9's Gordie Howe Hat Tricks came during the 1953–54 season.

The first one came on October 11, 1953, when Howe scored a goal, had an assist on Red Kelly's goal, and fought Fernie Flaman of the Toronto Maple Leafs. The other came on March 21, 1954, also against the Maple Leafs. This time, Howe scored the game's first goal, assisted on two goals by linemate Ted Lindsay, and had a fight with Ted "Teeder" Kennedy.

12 The Red Wings have had 279 games, 253 in the regular season, 26 in the Stanley Cup Playoffs in which a player has scored three or more goals. In 1999–2000, the Red Wings had just one hat trick during the regular season and one in the playoffs—and each belonged to Martin Lapointe, who got them less than a month apart.

Lapointe entered the Red Wings' game against the New York Rangers at Joe Louis Arena on March 26, 2000, with 12 goals. His career best was 16, which he'd achieved twice in the previous three seasons. He was a guy who played about 14 to 15 minutes a game, a checker who could contribute some goals but earned his money shutting down opponents.

On this night, Lapointe got the Red Wings off to a fast start when he scored against Mike Richter at 3:12 of the first period. The Rangers tied the game soon after on a goal by Brian Leetch, but the Red Wings blew the game open during the first half of the second period when goals by Brendan Shanahan, Steve Yzerman, and Sergei Fedorov made it 4–1.

At 12:21, Lapointe scored his second of the night to give the Red Wings a 5–1 lead. He completed the first hat trick of his NHL career at 15:24, beating Richter for the third time to make it 6–1. The three goals came on three shots. An assist on Nicklas Lidstrom's third-period power-play goal gave Lapointe a four-point night and an 8–2 win.

Lapointe scored one more goal during the regular season and finished with 16 for the third time in four seasons.

The Red Wings faced the Los Angeles Kings in the Western Conference Quarterfinals and began the series with a 2–0 win. Game 2, on April 15 at Joe Louis Arena, was much more wide open, and it turned into another big night for Lapointe.

After Shanahan put the Red Wings ahead 55 seconds into the game, Lapointe made it 2–0 when he scored at 1:33. The Wings led, 3–2, and were on a power play, when Lapointe scored again at 6:56 for a 4–2 lead.

The back-and-forth scoring continued into the second period, and with LA's Kelly Buchberger off for charging, Lapointe completed his hat trick with a power-play goal at 9:33, giving Detroit a 6–3 lead. It proved to be the game-winner in a wild 8–5 victory that gave Detroit a 2–0 lead in a series the Wings went on to sweep.

Those were the Red Wings' only hat tricks in 1999–2000, and Lapointe's only two with Detroit. He had one more in his NHL career, with the Boston Bruins against the New Jersey Devils on March 13, 2003.

13 He's almost forgotten today, but Ebbie Goodfellow was one of Detroit's early stars, whether the franchise was known as the Cougars, Falcons, or Red Wings.

Goodfellow came to the NHL with the Detroit Cougars as a forward in 1929–30 and was an instant success, finishing with 17 goals and 34 points in 44 games. He had 25 goals and 48 points in 44 games in his second season, and he was a consistent scorer, reaching double figures in goals in each of his first six seasons.

The NHL added the penalty shot to its rule book for the 1934–35 season, allowing referees to award them when a player was fouled "in good scoring position." In the first season, the shot was taken from a circle 38 feet from the net, and goaltenders had to be stationary until the shot was taken.

Goodfellow was the first member of the Red Wings to be awarded a penalty shot. It came during a game against the New York Rangers on November 15, 1934, and he failed to score against goaltender Percy Jackson.

Goodfellow had another chance a week later, again against the Rangers, but was denied by goaltender Andy Aitkenhead.

The third time was the charm. Goodfellow was awarded a penalty shot against the St. Louis Eagles and beat goaltender Bill Beveridge for the first penalty-shot goal in Red Wings history.

Though Goodfellow had three more penalty shots during the remainder of the season, he was unable to score; Alex Connell of the Montreal Maroons stopped him twice, and Dave Kerr of the Rangers denied him once.

Goodfellow had the Red Wings' only two penalty shots in 1935–36, but he couldn't beat George Hainsworth of the Toronto Maple

Leafs on November 24 or Tiny Thompson of the Boston Bruins on December 29.

It took until the third season of the penalty shot before a Red Wing other than Goodfellow took one. John Sorrell was awarded a penalty shot on December 25, 1936, but he was unable to beat Chicago's Mike Karakas.

Goodfellow didn't get another penalty shot until December 17, 1939, when he was unable to beat Kerr in a game against the Rangers that ended in a scoreless tie. His last chance came on February 13, 1940, when he scored against Frank Brimsek of the Bruins in a 10–3 loss at Boston Garden.

14 In the early 1950s, Gordie Howe practically owned the Art Ross Trophy, first awarded after the 1947–48 season to the player who led the NHL in scoring during the regular season. Howe won it for the first time in 1950–51 and repeated in each of the next three seasons. He won again in 1956–57 and 1962–63, giving him an NHL-record six. That mark lasted until Wayne Gretzky won the Art Ross 10 times in the 1980s and early 1990s. Mario Lemieux tied Howe for second place with six scoring titles, and Phil Esposito and Jaromir Jagr each won the Art Ross five times.

Howe wasn't the first Red Wing to win the Art Ross Trophy. That honor, for the 1949–50 season, went to Ted Lindsay, who, along with Howe and center Sid Abel, formed the "Production Line."

With the season expanded to 70 games, Lindsay scored 23 goals and led the NHL with 55 assists and 78 points. Lindsay led a 1–2–3 sweep by the Red Wings' top line. Abel was second with 69 points and Howe came in third with 68. Not surprisingly, the Red Wings were the runaway league leader in goals scored with 229, 26 more than the runner-up Chicago Black Hawks.

Though Lindsay was a First-Team All-Star six times in the next seven seasons and had a career-best 85 points in 1956–57, he never won the Art Ross again—and no Red Wing has won it since Howe in 1962–63.

15 The Red Wings struggled to score for much of the 2017–18 season, so it's not surprising that no Detroit player was able to get a hat trick.

It was just the third time since the NHL expanded from six teams to 12 in 1967–68 that the Red Wings had no player score three goals in a game.

The first came in 1970–71, Gordie Howe's final season and one in which the Red Wings managed just 209 goals, the fewest in the East Division and the fourth-lowest total in the NHL. Tom Webster led the Wings with 30 goals and had five two-goal games. Howe was second with 23 and scored two goals in a game twice. Alex Delvecchio (21), was the only other Detroit player to break 20 goals, and he also had a pair of two-goal games.

The other no-hat-trick season is a lot more surprising.

The Red Wings led the NHL in scoring during the 2008–09 season with 295 goals on the way to finishing first in the Western Conference and second in the NHL with 112 points (the Boston Bruins were first with 116). Marian Hossa led Detroit with 40 goals, followed by Johan Franzen (34), Pavel Datsyuk (32), and Henrik Zetterberg (31). Jiri Hudler scored 23 goals and Mikael Samuelsson 19.

The Red Wings led the NHL in power-play percentage (25.5) and power-play goals scored. They took more shots than anyone in the NHL (2,965) and allowed the second-fewest (2,274).

The only thing that 2008–09 team couldn't do was get a hat trick. Hossa had eight two-goal games, including back-to-back games on February 2 and 4, but couldn't get three. Neither could Franzen (four two-goal games), Datsyuk (six), or Zetterberg (four).

16 Gordie Howe was a fixture on the NHL's postseason All-Star teams for two decades. He was a Second-Team All-Star in 1949 and 1950, moved up to the First-Team All-Star in 1951, and missed making one or the other just twice through 1970. He was a First-Team All-Star for the third straight season in 1969–70, earning the nod not long after his 42nd birthday. In all, he made it 21 times, an NHL record that's not likely to be broken.

Before Howe, the only Detroit right wing to have made an All-Star team was Larry Aurie, who was voted to the First-Team in 1937.

Perhaps surprisingly, the Red Wings have had just one right wing voted as an All-Star in the nearly five decades since Howe's final game with the Wings in 1971.

The Red Wings obtained Mickey Redmond from the Montreal Canadiens on January 13, 1971, along with forwards Bill Collins and Guy Charron, for left wing Frank Mahovlich. Coming to Detroit, where Howe was in his final season with the Red Wings, turned out to be just what Redmond needed for his career to take off.

Redmond had never scored more than 27 goals in a season until 1971–72, his first with the Red Wings, when he fired home 42. He was even better in 1972–73, pumping home 52 goals and finishing with 93 points. He finished sixth in the voting for the Hart Trophy and beat out former Montreal teammate Yvan Cournoyer to earn a berth on the NHL's First All-Star Team.

In 1973–74, Redmond showed his 52-goal season was no fluke by scoring 51 times and finishing with 77 points. Ken Hodge of the Boston Bruins was voted a First-Team All-Star, and Redmond was selected to the Second Team.

No Detroit right wing has made a postseason All-Star team since then. Mike Foligno, Johan Franzen, and Johan Garpenlov all had some excellent seasons with the Wings, but none was good enough to make a postseason All-Star team.

Injuries cut Redmond's playing career short. Today he's a fixture on telecasts of Red Wings' games.

17 The Red Wings have had 18 goaltenders play at least 100 games, and nine of them earned at least 100 victories while wearing the winged wheel. They include three members of the Hockey Hall of Fame: Terry Sawchuk (352), Harry Lumley (163), and Dominik Hasek (114). Chris Osgood, who's second to Sawchuk with 317 victories and had 401 overall, could get there some day, while Roger Crozier (131), Tim Cheveldae (128), and Manny Legace (112) were part of winning teams with Detroit. Jimmy Howard (221) is in his

Jimmy Howard passed the 200-win mark during the 2017–18 season. (Photo By Anna Enriquez—Flickr: Jimmy Howard; License: CC BY 2.0; Source: https://commons.wikimedia.org/w/index.php?curid=15989969)

second decade with the Wings and surpassed the 200-win mark in 2017–18.

All eight of those goalies finished with or have more wins than regulation losses.

Not so with the one other 100-game winner in Wings history.

Greg Stefan had the misfortune to play during the high-scoring 1980s, when defense took a back seat to offense. In addition, the Wings were in a down phase during most of Stefan's time in Detroit.

The Red Wings took Stefan in the seventh round (No. 128) in the 1981 NHL Draft. Amazingly, he was in the NHL less than a year later, and was 0–2–0, allowing 10 goals, on a team that went 21–47–12 and was outscored 351–270. None of the five goaltenders who played for Detroit that season had a winning record.

Stefan led the Wings with 35 games played in 1981–82, but he was 6–16–9 with a 4.52 goals-against average for a team that went 21–44–15. The Wings improved to 31–42–7 the following season, and Stefan cut his GAA by more than one goal per game, finishing 19–22–2 with a 3.51 goals-against average.

He had his first winning season in 1984–85, going 21–19–2 despite a 4.33 GAA. After going 10–20–5 in 1985–86, Stefan had three straight winning seasons, and he earned a few Vezina Trophy votes in 1987–88 by going 17–9–5 with a 3.11 goals-against average.

Stefan got off to a slow start in 1989–90, going 1–5–0 in his first six decisions, before injuring his knee in a game against the Edmonton Oilers on November 25, 1989. He had surgery but never played in the NHL again.

Stefan's 115–127–30 record makes him the only goaltender in Wings history with more than 100 victories who finished with a losing record.

18 The Red Wings and the Lady Byng Trophy, given each season to the player who exhibits the best combination of skillful and gentlemanly play, have a long history together.

Beginning in 1937, when it was won by forward Marty Berry after a season in which he had 17 goals, 44 points, six penalty minutes, and was named a First-Team All-Star for a team that won the Stanley Cup, seven Red Wings have won the Lady Byng a total of 14 times. Two of the three defensemen to win the award were Red Wings: Bill Quackenbush, who took home the Lady Byng in 1948–49—and then was quickly traded by general manager Jack Adams, who thought the trophy meant he wasn't tough enough—and Red Kelly, who won it in 1950–51, 1952–53, and 1953–54. Kelly also won the Lady Byng in 1960–61, but by then he was with a different team (the Toronto Maple Leafs) and playing a different position (center).

Center Alex Delvecchio won the Lady Byng three times, in

1958–59, 1965–66, and 1968–69. That came after Dutch Reibel won it in 1955–56.

Marcel Dionne took home the Lady Byng in 1974–75, a season in which he had 47 goals, 121 points, and 14 penalty minutes. He won it again two years later while playing with the Los Angeles Kings.

The Red Wings didn't have another Lady Byng winner for more than 30 years, but Pavel Datsyuk more than made up for lost time. He won the Lady Byng in 2005–06, when he had 28 goals, 87 points and 22 penalty minutes, then won it again in 2006–07, again finishing with 87 points, while taking just 20 minutes in penalties.

Datsyuk bumped up his offensive production to 97 points in each of the next two seasons, while taking 20 and 22 minutes in penalties, winning the Lady Byng for the third and fourth times. His streak ended in 2009–10, when he finished third behind Martin St. Louis and Brad Richards of the Tampa Bay Lightning.

Datsyuk and Kelly each won the Lady Byng four times. Only Frank Boucher (seven) and Wayne Gretzky (five) have more. Datsyuk and Boucher are the only players to win the trophy in four consecutive seasons.

19 The NHL conducted a massive project during 2017, its centennial year, that resulted in scoresheets from the league's entire 100-year history being computerized and checked for accuracy. Some players had goals and points added or subtracted, and categories such as power-play, short-handed, winning, and tying goals were able to be determined accurately.

All that work enabled Wings fans to discover that Gordie Howe was the first player in franchise history to reach double figures in game-winning goals. He had 10 in 1951–52, when the Red Wings finished first during a 70-game season and went on to win the Stanley Cup.

No Detroit player reached double figures again until 1964–65, when another future Hall of Famer, center Norm Ullman, had 10 game-winners among his 42 goals.

It wasn't until 1993–94 that another Red Wing hit double figures in game-winners. On his way to winning the Hart Trophy, center Sergei Fedorov had 10 among his 56 goals.

Fedorov set the franchise record in 1995–96. Although he scored "only" 39 goals, 11 of them were game-winners, helping the Red Wings set an NHL record with 62 victories. Fedorov matched his team record seven years later, when 11 of his 36 goals stood as game-winners.

Two players have come close to matching Fedorov's mark since then. Henrik Zetterberg scored 10 game-winners in 2006–07, when he had 33 goals. Johan Franzen is the most recent to hit double figures. Ten of his 29 goals in 2011–12 won games.

Howe has the all-time franchise record with 121 game-winners, with Steve Yzerman next at 94, and Fedorov third with 79.

20 There were a lot of things that made Nicklas Lidstrom a Hall of Famer. He was an excellent skater, a brilliant power-play quarterback, had a knack for getting his shots through to the net for goals or to generate rebounds for teammates, and was superb in his own zone. But perhaps the best thing about Lidstrom was that he was able to play at such a high level for nearly half the game—and do it almost every season.

In a span of 10 seasons, from 1997–98 through 2007–08 (noting that the 2004–05 season was wiped out by the lockout), Lidstrom missed a total of 15 games while playing an average of at least 26:30 per game in each of those seasons. His busiest season was 2002–03, when he played all 82 games, finished with 18 goals and 62 points, and averaged a league-leading 29:20 of ice time. That was 32 seconds more per game than he'd averaged the previous season. In fact, during a span of four seasons from 1999–2000 through 2002–03, Lidstrom averaged at least 28:26 of ice time per game, a stretch in which he scored 59 to 73 points per season and was a First-Team All-Star each time.

Lidstrom's 10-season streak of averaging at least 26:30 per game began when he averaged 27:14 in 1997–98, helping the Red Wings retain the Stanley Cup. His lowest average ice time during the streak came in 1998–99 (26:30); the next time he averaged less than 27 minutes per game was in 2007–08 (26:43).

Larry Murphy, Lidstrom's defense partner for much of the late 1990s, has the highest average time on ice per game in a season for anyone other than No. 5. Murphy, also a Hockey Hall of Famer, averaged 25:50 per game in 1997–98.

Chris Chelios averaged more than 25 minutes a game twice for the Red Wings (25:16 in 1999–2000, 25:18 in 2001–02). Niklas Kronwall's busiest season came in 2012–13, when he averaged 24:21 while playing all 48 games during a lockout-shortened season. He averaged 24:18 in 2013–14, his highest total during a full season.

21 Hall of Famers Syd Howe, Ted Lindsay, and Brendan Shanahan are among the eight Red Wings who share the franchise record for career overtime goals in the Stanley Cup Playoffs with two. Mud Bruneteau, Johan Franzen, Vyacheslav Kozlov, and Kirk Maltby also have scored two OT goals in the playoffs.

But none of them scored twice in overtime during the same playoff year. The only Red Wing to do that was Leo Reise Jr.

The nine-year NHL veteran was born while his father, Leo Sr., was playing in the 1920s with the Hamilton Tigers, New York Americans, and New York Rangers during his own eight-year NHL career. Leo Jr. followed in his footsteps, becoming part of the first father-son tandem to play in the NHL.

After splitting two seasons between the Chicago Black Hawks and the minors, Leo Jr. joined the Red Wings in 1946–47. He played six seasons with Detroit and was a key part of two Stanley Cup championship teams, despite getting a lot less attention on a defense corps that included "Black Jack" Stewart, Marcel Pronovost, Red Kelly, and Bill Quackenbush.

Reise scored a spectacular short-handed goal in Game 7 of the 1949 Semifinals against the Montreal Canadiens that broke a tie and helped the Red Wings to a 3–1 victory. He gathered the puck in his own zone and battled along the boards past all five Montreal skaters, before beating Canadiens goalie Bill Durnan with a 40-foot shot.

That was just a warmup for his heroics in 1950.

The Red Wings finished first in the regular season in 1949–50, but the three-time defending Stanley Cup champion Toronto Maple Leafs led, 2–1, in their semifinal series entering Game 4 at Maple Leaf Gardens. The teams were tied, 1–1, and had played a scoreless overtime period before Reise took a backhander that hit the leg of Leafs defenseman Gus Mortson and went past goalie Turk Broda 38 seconds into the second overtime for a 2–1 victory.

The Red Wings lost Game 5 at home but kept their hopes alive by winning, 4–0, in Game 6 at Toronto. Game 7 was scoreless through three periods, but at 8:39 of OT, Reise lifted a 35-foot backhander that went through a crowd of bodies and sailed past Broda to put the Red Wings into the Final, where they defeated the New York Rangers in seven games to win the Cup.

Needless to say, the two overtime goals ranked as his career highlight.

"I think it has to be the year we won the Stanley Cup in '49–'50, when I scored the two overtime goals against the Toronto Maple Leafs to eliminate them out of the Semifinals," he told GreatestHockeyLegends.com. "It was a pretty rough series. I think those goals I scored in overtime were probably the highlights."

Reise was part of Detroit's 1952 championship team, then played two seasons with the Rangers before leaving the NHL after the 1953–54 season.

22 Steve Yzerman had to settle for second place on the Red Wings' all-time scoring list behind Gordie Howe. He had 1,755 points in 22 seasons, while Howe finished his 25 seasons in Detroit with 1,809 points. But with some help from more rounds in the postseason, Yzerman is on top of the heap when it comes to playoff scoring.

The Red Wings qualified for the Stanley Cup Playoffs 20 times during Yzerman's 22-season career, and in his 196 postseason games he piled up 185 points: 70 goals and 115 assists. (The 70 goals are also a Wings' playoff record.)

Yzerman had three goals and six points in four games during his first trip to the playoffs in 1984. His first big showing in the postseason came in 1987, when he helped the Wings advance to the Campbell Conference Final by scoring five goals and finishing with 18 points in 16 games.

Yzerman reached 20 points in a single postseason for the first of three times in 1996, when he had eight goals and 20 points in 18 games. After putting up seven goals and 13 points in 20 games during Detroit's run to the Stanley Cup in 1997, he had his most productive postseason in 1998, leading all players with 18 assists and 24 points, fueling Detroit's second straight championship. That performance earned him the Conn Smythe Trophy as playoff MVP.

Though the Wings were upset in the second round in 1999, Yzerman scored a career-best nine goals in 10 games. His last big postseason came in 2002, when the Red Wings won the Cup for the third time in five seasons. He scored six goals and had 23 points in 22 games.

Yzerman scored his last three playoff goals in 2004, moving him past Howe (67) for the franchise playoff record. He had four assists in four games during the 2006 postseason before retiring.

With 185 points, Yzerman has two more than longtime teammate Nicklas Lidstrom, whose 183 points include a franchise-record 129 assists. Another longtime teammate, Sergei Fedorov, is third with 163, followed by Howe with 158 in 154 games.

23 The NHL did away with ties beginning with the 2005–06 season, when the league adopted the shootout to settle games that remained deadlocked after a five-minute overtime.

The Red Wings played at least four ties in every season from 1926–27 through 2003–04, with a single-season high of 18 in 1952–53, 1980–81, and 1996–97 (they won the Stanley Cup at the end of the first and last of those three seasons).

Of all the teams the Red Wings played before 2004, the only one they never had a game end in a tie with was the Atlanta Thrashers, now the Winnipeg Jets. The Thrashers entered the NHL in the 1999–2000 season and faced the Red Wings seven times through 2003–04. The Red Wings won all seven. In all, they've played 24 times through the

2017–18; the Red Wings are 14–8 with two overtime losses. Detroit was 8–3 with two overtime losses at home and 6–5–0 on the road.

In contrast, the Red Wings and New York Rangers played 103 ties, the most of any opponent. The Red Wings, then known as the Cougars, played their first tie against the Rangers in their second meeting, ending at 1–1 on December 19, 1926, at Madison Square Garden. The season with the most ties between the teams was 1959–60, when six of the 14 games between the Red Wings and Rangers ended without a winner (four of them ended 3–3, the others finished 2–2).

The 103rd and final tie between the Red Wings and Rangers came on January 19, 1993, when the teams played to a 2–2 draw at Joe Louis Arena. The Red Wings and Rangers played 17 times after that before the shootout was adopted, with Detroit winning 13 and losing four.

The highest-scoring of the 103 ties came on March 19, 1965, when the Red Wings and Rangers played to a 6–6 draw at Madison Square Garden, a game in which Detroit's Norm Ullman had a hat trick. The only scoreless tie between the teams came on December 17, 1939, at the Olympia, when neither Dave Kerr of the Rangers nor Tiny Thompson of the Wings allowed a goal in 70 minutes of play (overtime before World War II was 10 minutes and not sudden-death).

24 Terry Sawchuk is the runaway leader in games played by a Red Wings goaltender, but he's nowhere near first place in points. In his 734 games and 43,646 minutes played for the Wings, Sawchuk was credited with just three assists.

Three goaltenders, Chris Osgood, Tim Cheveldae, and Greg Stefan, share the franchise record with 15 assists apiece.

Stefan had a seven-season "scoring streak," putting up at least one assist in each season from 1983–84 through 1989–90. His biggest season was 1986–87, when he was credited with four assists.

Cheveldae had 13 of his 15 assists with the Red Wings from 1990–91 through 1992–93. That included a franchise single-season-best five assists in 1990–91, with four in each of the next two seasons.

Osgood's 15 assists with the Wings were much more spread out. The first one came in 1995–96, the last in 2009–10. The biggest offensive season of his NHL career actually came when he had four assists with the New York Islanders in 2001–02; he never had more than three points in any season with Detroit. Still, Osgood is tops on the Wings' all-time scoring list for goaltenders because he did something that neither Stefan nor Cheveldae did: He scored a goal.

On March 6, 1996, Osgood shot the puck down the ice and into an empty net against the Hartford Whalers. With one goal and 15 assists, Osgood is the leading scorer among Red Wings goaltenders, with 16 points.

25 Dave Gagnon was a star during his three seasons at Colgate University, leading the Red Raiders to the NCAA championship game in 1990, when he was named the ECAC Player of the Year. He had never been drafted by an NHL team but was signed by the Red Wings on June 11, 1990.

Gagnon split most of the season between the Adirondack Red Wings of the AHL and Hampton Roads of the ECHL. But he also got a callup from the Wings and made his NHL debut against the St. Louis Blues at Joe Louis Arena on January 25, 1991, in what turned out to be a historic night.

The Blues lit up Tim Cheveldae for seven goals in the first two periods. The last of those goals was by St. Louis star Brett Hull, his 49th of the season in the Blues' 49th game. With the outcome no longer in doubt, Detroit coach Bryan Murray inserted Gagnon to start the third period.

Hull had scored No. 49 late in the second period during a five-minute power play that carried into the third period. He gave Gagnon a rude welcome to the NHL, by taking a pass from Adam Oates and beating Gagnon with a wrist shot from the slot 1:30 into the third period. That gave Hull 50 goals, allowing him to join Wayne Gretzky and Mario Lemieux as the only players in NHL history at that time to score 50 in less than 50 games.

"It's hard to explain how much it means to me," Hull said. "If you look at the guys who have done it, and the guys who haven't, it's pretty amazing company."

If nothing else, it left Gagnon with a memorable NHL debut.

"I've been waiting for this moment for my whole life, and now I'm in the record books," Gagnon said. "I should have had it. I was moving across from left to right, and the puck slid under me."

Gagnon gave up another goal on the same power play to Geoff Courtnall, but he stopped 16 other shots in what turned out to be a 9–4 loss for the Wings.

Three nights later, Gagnon made his second and final NHL appearance. In his only NHL start, he was lifted after surrendering four goals on 10 shots in a 6–2 loss to the New Jersey Devils. His career NHL line: 35 minutes played, an 0–1–0 record, 10.29 goals-against average, and a save percentage of .786.

Though Gagnon never played in the NHL again, he spent another 10 seasons in the minor leagues before retiring in 2001. He was named MVP of the Kelly Cup playoffs in 1994, when he led the Toledo Storm to the ECHL championship.

26 Terry Sawchuk established himself as one of the NHL's greatest goaltenders during the first half of the 1950s, helping the Red Wings win the Stanley Cup in 1952, 1954, and 1955 while finishing with a goals-against average of less than 2.00 for five straight seasons.

Sawchuk also set a franchise record in 1951–52 by posting 12 shutouts, then matched that mark in 1953–54 and again in 1954–55. But general manager Jack Adams traded Sawchuk to the Boston Bruins in the summer of 1955, to make room for another talented young goaltender.

Glenn Hall stepped into the starter's role for the 1955–56 season and was almost as good as Sawchuk, finishing with a 2.18 GAA and matching Sawchuk's franchise record with 12 shutouts. Hall played well in 1956–57, winning 38 regular-season games with a 2.21 GAA. But his shutouts dropped from 12 to four, and Adams traded him to the Chicago Black Hawks that summer, after reacquiring Sawchuk from the Bruins.

No Red Wings goaltender has come close to the record held by Sawchuk and Hall in the next six-plus decades. In fact, the Wings

Terry Sawchuk backstopped the Red Wings to the Stanley Cup in 1952, 1954, and 1955. (Associated Press)

haven't had double figures in shutouts since Hall's 12 in 1955–56. Dominik Hasek's eight shutouts in 2006–07 are the most by any Detroit goaltender since then.

27 When the Brooklyn (formerly New York) Americans folded in 1942, the NHL was left with six teams. It stayed that way until 1967, when the Original Six era ended with the addition of six new teams.

The Red Wings, who had lost the Stanley Cup Final to the Toronto Maple Leafs in 1942, finished first in 1942–43, going 25–14–11 in the NHL's expanded 60-game schedule and winning the Cup for the third time in franchise history.

The Wings qualified for the Stanley Cup Playoffs in each of the next 15 seasons. They set an NHL record by finishing first in the regular-season standings for seven consecutive seasons (1948–49 through 1954–55) and they won the Stanley Cup four times in six seasons (1949–50 through 1954–55).

But all good things come to an end, and so it did for the Wings. They finished second in 1955–56 and lost to the Montreal Canadiens in the Final, came in first in 1956–57 but were upset by the Boston Bruins in the Semifinals, and were bounced again in the 1958 Semifinals after coming in third.

Still, there was no reason to believe the Red Wings wouldn't be back in the playoffs in 1959. This was, after all, a team that had three Hall of Famers at forward (Gordie Howe, Norm Ullman, and Alex Delvecchio), two more on defense (Marcel Pronovost and Red Kelly), and a legendary goaltender (Terry Sawchuk).

Detroit lost its season opener, 2–0, to the Canadiens at the Forum, then won four of its next five games. But the Wings just drifted for the remainder of the season. Their longest losing streak was five games, and they neither won more than three in a row nor went longer than four games without losing.

The Red Wings' biggest problem was their inability to handle the Canadiens. Detroit went 1–9–4 against Montreal. The Wings allowed seven or more goals in five of the losses and were shut out three times. The only victory came on January 29, 1959, when they won 4–1 at the Forum.

Detroit also went 0–6–1 in its final seven games against the Bruins. The Red Wings won just one season series, edging the Chicago Black Hawks, 7–6–1.

When the season ended with a 6–4 loss to the Toronto Maple Leafs on March 22, the Red Wings had finished last for the first time since 1934–35. With a 25–37–8 record, they finished six points behind the fifth-place New York Rangers. Detroit scored a league-low 167 goals and allowed 218, the most in the NHL, and its minus-51 differential was by far the worst in the NHL (no other team was worse than minus-16).

The Wings rebounded to finish third in 1959–60, and they made the playoffs six times in a span of seven seasons before coming in fifth in 1966–67, the final season of the Original Six era. They finished last in the East Division in 1967–68 and again in 1970–71, all part of a 17-season stretch in which they made the playoffs just twice.

28 The second golden era for the Red Wings began in the early 1990s and lasted through the first decade of the 21st century. That span included four seasons (1996–97, 1997–96, 2001–02, and 2007–08) in which Detroit won the Stanley Cup, and two others (1994–95 and 2008–09) in which they advanced to the Final.

In the 15 seasons from 1993–94 through 2008–09, the Red Wings finished first in their division 12 times and second in the other three. From 2000–01 through 2008–09, they finished first in eight straight seasons (the 2004–05 season was cancelled because of a lockout).

Perhaps surprisingly, the Red Wings finished first in only two of the four seasons that ended in a Stanley Cup celebration. The Wings finished first in 1993–94, 1994–95, and 1995–96, but came up empty each time. The 1995–96 team set a franchise record with 131 points but lost the Western Conference Final to the Colorado Avalanche.

The 1996–97 season was just the opposite. The Red Wings finished second in the Central Division with a 38–26–18 record, and their 94 points left them 10 behind the first-place Dallas Stars. But in the playoffs, the Wings defeated the St. Louis Blues in six games, swept the Mighty Ducks of Anaheim, ousted the defending Stanley Cup champion Avalanche in six games, then swept the Philadelphia Flyers in the Final to win the Cup for the first time since 1955.

The Wings improved to 44–23–15 in 1997–98, though they still finished second in the Central Division behind the Dallas Stars. However, they defeated the Phoenix Coyotes, the Blues, and the Stars, each in six games, before sweeping the Washington Capitals in the Final.

Detroit finished first in two of the next three seasons but didn't get back to the Stanley Cup Final. However, the 2001–02 team finished first in the overall NHL standings at 51–17 with 10 ties and four overtime losses, then defeated the Vancouver Canucks in six games and the

Blues in five before outlasting the defending champion Avalanche in seven games to win the Western Conference Final. The Red Wings lost the opener of the Stanley Cup Final to the Carolina Hurricanes, but won the next four games for their third championship in six seasons.

The Red Wings finished first overall again in 2007–08 with 115 points (54–21–7) and never trailed in any of their four playoff series. Detroit polished off the Nashville Predators in six games, swept Colorado, and defeated Dallas in six games before knocking off the Pittsburgh Penguins in six games to win the Cup.

Detroit won its division again and finished third overall in 2008–09, then defeated the Columbus Blue Jackets, Anaheim Ducks, and Chicago Blackhawks to get back to the Final, but lost to Pittsburgh in seven games.

29 The Red Wings are probably glad the New York Islanders have been the guests at their New Year's Eve festivities just twice, because the team from Long Island spoiled the party each time.

The Islanders still had the core of their dynasty team when they came to Joe Louis Arena on December 31, 1985. Meanwhile, the Red Wings were on their way to a last-place finish (17–57–6). After allowing an early goal to Bryan Trottier, the Red Wings scored three times and led, 3–1, after one period. Steve Yzerman scored 50 seconds after Trottier's goal, and Ron Duguay beat Kelly Hrudey twice in 50 seconds midway through the period.

Mike Bossy's goal late in the second period made it 3–2, but it looked like there would be a Happy New Year for Detroit fans when Lane Lambert scored early in the third period for a 4–2 lead. However, goals by Stefan Persson and Paul Boutilier tied the game, 4–4, and Mikko Makela's goal 53 seconds into overtime gave New York a 5–4 win. Under the rules at the time, the Wings went home empty-handed—there were no three-point games.

The circumstances were reversed when the Islanders came to the Joe on New Year's Eve in 2010. The Red Wings were again among the NHL's elite, while the Islanders had finished last in the NHL the previous season and would miss the playoffs again.

The course of the game was also reversed. Johan Franzen gave Detroit an early lead before Matt Moulson and John Tavares put the Islanders ahead, 2–1, after the first period. Jesse Joensuu made it 3–1 late in the second period, but Valtteri Filppula's goal with nine seconds remaining cut the deficit to 3–2 after two periods, and Tomas Tatar's goal midway through the third period got the Wings even.

The Red Wings failed to capitalize on a power play early in overtime, and then the Islanders took advantage of a holding penalty against Henrik Zetterberg to score the game-winner, with PA Parenteau's power-play goal at 3:57 giving the Islanders a 4–3 win.

The Red Wings fared better in their other two overtime games on New Year's Eve, defeating the Ottawa Senators, 5–4, in 1992, and the Atlanta Thrashers, 6–5, in 2003.

30 Five of the 10 men who've served as general manager of the Red Wings are members of the Hockey Hall of Fame, but only three are in the Hall because of their playing career with the Red Wings.

Jack Adams was inducted into the Hall as a player, but his playing career ended before he came to the Wings as general manager and coach in 1927. Adams held both jobs through 1947, when he stepped down from coaching to concentrate on his role as general manager, a job he held until 1962.

Jim Devellano was the first hire by Mike Ilitch after Ilitch bought the Red Wings in 1982. He served as GM through the 1989–90 season, was bumped upstairs when Brian Murray became GM in 1990, then returned to the general manager's office after the 1993–94 season. Devellano was moved upstairs again when Ken Holland was named GM in 1997, serving as a senior vice president and alternate governor.

The first former Red Wings star to become general manager was Sid Abel, who replaced Adams as GM. Abel had taken over as coach midway through the 1957–58 season after a playing career that would earn him induction into the Hall of Fame in 1969. Abel was named GM after Adams was fired and served as coach and GM through 1967–68, when he stepped down as coach in favor of Bill Gadsby.

Abel returned as coach two games into the 1969–70 season and led the Red Wings to the playoffs. Ned Harkness then took over as coach for the 1970–71 season with Abel as GM, but Harkness was promoted to GM midway through the season, replacing Abel, with Doug Barkley going behind the bench as coach.

Harkness was fired on February 6, 1974, and Delvecchio, who had been named coach after retiring as a player earlier in the season, added the general manager's job to his portfolio. Delvecchio was GM and spent a couple of stints doing both jobs until leaving the Red Wings for good on March 16, 1977.

Delvecchio's successor was Ted Lindsay, his longtime teammate and oft-times linemate. Soon after taking over as general manager, "Terrible Ted" appeared in TV commercials promoting the slogan "Aggressive hockey is back in town." The Red Wings made the play-offs in 1977–78 for the first time since 1970, and they won a series for the first time since 1965. For his efforts, Lindsay was voted the NHL's executive of the year. Late in the 1979–80 season, Lindsay named himself as coach and gave up the GM's role to Jimmy Skinner, but he was then forced out after the Wings started 3–14–3 in 1980–81.

31 Mike Babcock is a proud alumnus of McGill University, and he hasn't been shy about wearing a lucky tie honoring his Montreal-based alma mater.

Babcock first wore the McGill apparel in Game 5 of the 2007 Western Conference Semifinals, a 3–2 victory against the San Jose Sharks on April 28 that was televised across North America on NBC and TSN.

Babcock, who was captain and MVP of the Redmen when he played at McGill during the mid-1980s, also wore the crimson red silk tie for Detroit's game at Montreal on December 4, 2007.

By 2010, the tie had its own Facebook page, "Mike Babcock's McGill Tie." He wore a red McGill tie while coaching Canada to the gold medal at the 2010 Vancouver Olympics, then sported a special black McGill tie when guiding Canada to gold four years later in Sochi, Russia. According to the *Montreal Gazette*, it was the same tie Babcock had worn when he'd received an honorary law doctorate from McGill in 2013.

He again wore a McGill tie while coaching Canada to victory at the World Cup of Hockey in 2016. According to McGill, the World Cup win improved his record when wearing a McGill tie to 9–4, including two Olympic gold medal games, one Stanley Cup, and the World Cup.

32 There's a good chance you know Dave Hanson more for what he did on the silver screen than on the ice at Joe Louis Arena.

Hanson, Detroit's 11th-round pick in the 1975 NHL Draft, had a cup of coffee with the Wings during the 1978–79 season, playing in 11 games and piling up 26 penalty minutes, but no points. He later played 22 games with the Minnesota North Stars, scoring his lone NHL goal.

"The opportunity to go with such a storied franchise as the Red Wings was, at that time, for me just a great feeling thinking there was going to be a shot for me to play in the National Hockey League," Hanson told the Red Wings website in 2012.

But before his time with the Wings, Hanson made a big impression in Hollywood.

Hanson was playing for the Johnstown Jets of the low-level North American Hockey League when a teammate's sister wrote a screenplay about the team's junior hockey experience. When it turned out that actors couldn't skate well enough to star in the movie, entitled *Slap Shot*, Hanson and the Carlson brothers, Jack, Jeff, and Steve, were cast as themselves—the three fictional Hanson brothers. When Jack Carlson was called up to the Edmonton Oilers, Dave "Killer" Hanson himself stepped in to complete the trio of brothers, while another actor, Jerry Houser, took over Dave's character in the movie.

Jack and Steve Carlson were originally drafted by the Red Wings in the mid-1970s but never played for them. Hanson did realize his dream.

"They plucked me from one part and threw me into the third brother, and the rest is cinematic history," Hanson told the Wings website. "It was three months of some of the best and most fun times that we've ever had. They gave us all the food we could eat and all the beer we could drink, and we pretended to be hockey players."

The film, which starred Paul Newman, took just three months to complete and has become a classic. Hanson said he was never worried about its success.

"There was no doubt in my mind," he said. "Besides the good looks of Paul Newman, you had three good-looking Hanson brothers. The chicks love the glasses."

By the time he made the NHL, Hanson was far better known than the average rookie.

"The role that I played on the hockey team, I wasn't exactly a fan favorite," Hanson said. "But when I went into opposing arenas, it was common now to suddenly be skating around in warm-ups and look up and see an entire section with the glasses and the fake noses. You had to just laugh, it was good stuff."

The original Hanson brothers were resurrected 25 years later when *Slap Shot 2: Breaking the Ice* was released in 2002. Another sequel, *Slap Shot 3: The Junior League*, came out six years later.

33 Gordie Howe, Guy Lafleur, and Mario Lemieux are three of hockey's immortals. Though their styles of play and accomplishments were different, they do have one thing in common: Each returned to play in the NHL after being inducted into the Hockey Hall of Fame.

Howe was first. He retired from the NHL in 1971 after 25 seasons with the Red Wings. The Hall of Fame waived its customary three-year waiting period and inducted Mr. Hockey in 1972. But with his sons just then old enough to play pro hockey, and the wrist injury that plagued him during his final season with the Wings healed, Howe opted to return and skate with his sons. The three joined the Houston Aeros of the World Hockey Association.

Howe averaged 100 points during his first three seasons with the Aeros. He played one more season with Houston and two with the New England Whalers before the NHL absorbed four WHA teams (including the Whalers) for the 1979–80 season. At age 51, Howe played all 80 games for the renamed Hartford Whalers, finishing with 15 goals and 41 points. He also had a goal and an assist in three playoff games before finally calling it a career.

Lafleur, a star in the 1970s and early 1980s for the Montreal Canadiens, retired in late 1984. Unlike Howe, he had to go through the Hall of Fame's waiting period before being elected in 1988—just before returning to the NHL with the New York Rangers. After not playing for nearly four years, Lafleur had 18 goals and 45 points for the Rangers, then spent two more seasons with the Quebec Nordiques before retiring for good.

By the time Lafleur called it a career, Lemieux was arguably the best player in the NHL. Health issues forced him to miss the 1994–95 season and to retire in 1997 after leading the NHL in scoring with 122 points. The Hall of Fame again waived its waiting period and inducted Lemieux a few months after his retirement. But he returned to the NHL midway through the 2000–01 season and didn't retire for good until early in the 2005–06 season.

34 Jack Adams is the only man in history to win the Stanley Cup as a player, coach, and general manager, though the award that carries his name today honors the NHL's coach of the year.

Adams was actually inducted into the Hockey Hall of Fame as a player. He began by playing two seasons with the Toronto Arenas (the future Maple Leafs), starred for three seasons with the Vancouver Millionaires of the Pacific Coast Hockey Association, returned to the NHL with Toronto (now known as the St. Patricks), and helped the Ottawa Senators win the Stanley Cup in 1926–27, his final season.

Adams went directly from playing to coaching when he took over the Detroit Cougars in 1927–28. He also served as general manager. He led Detroit to the Stanley Cup Playoffs for the first time in 1928–29. The renamed Red Wings won their first division title in 1933–34, and two seasons later again finished first in the American Division under Adams before winning its first Stanley Cup championship.

At that time, the NHL selected First-Team and Second-Team coaches, along with its postseason All-Star teams. Adams didn't win either, despite Detroit's performance in 1935–36, but when the Red Wings again won the American Division and led the NHL in points before repeating as champion in 1936–37, Adams was selected as First-Team All-Star coach for the first time.

The Red Wings missed the playoffs in 1937–38 and didn't get back to the Stanley Cup Final until 1941, when they were swept by the Boston Bruins. They made the Final again the following season after going 19–25–4 during the regular season, then became the first team to lose the Final after winning the first three games of the series.

The Red Wings made the 1942 Stanley Cup Final against the Toronto Maple Leafs despite having a losing record in the regular season. (Conn Smythe Fonds—This image is available from the Archives of Ontario under the item reference code F 223-3-2-7-5; Source: https://commons.wikimedia.org/w/index .php?curid=3487535)

But there was no stopping the Wings in 1942–43. They finished first in the six-team NHL, then defeated the Toronto Maple Leafs in six games in the Semifinals before sweeping the Boston Bruins in the Final. Adams was honored as the First-Team All-Star coach for the second and final time.

Adams coached the Red Wings for four more seasons, earning Second-Team honors in 1944–45, before stepping down as coach after the 1946–47 season to concentrate on his role as general manager, a job he held until 1963.

35 The Kharlamov Trophy was established by Sovetsky Sport for the 2002–02 season. It's named for Valeri Kharlamov, a star for the Soviet National Team in the 1970s who became known worldwide after a brilliant performance in the 1972 Summit Series against Team Canada, a team comprised of top players in the NHL. The award is presented each summer in Moscow.

Until 2015, only NHL players were eligible for the award. Voting took place at the conclusion of each season. Every Russian-born player who had played at least one game in the NHL during that season would be allowed to name his top three picks (they could not vote for themselves).

Starting with 2015–16, voting participation and eligibility rules were changed. Russian players from the NHL and Kontinental Hockey League (KHL) were made eligible. A short list of the 20 best players from the two leagues is compiled, then voted on by a selection committee composed of five groups of experts, each consisting of 13 individuals, plus past award winners.

The very first winner was a Red Wing.

Though Detroit was upset by the Mighty Ducks of Anaheim in the first round of the Stanley Cup Playoffs, Wings center Sergei Fedorov finished the 2002–03 season with 36 goals and 83 points, his best offensive numbers since 1995–96. That was enough to make him the first player honored with the Kharlamov Trophy.

After Ilya Kovalchuk won in 2004 and Alex Ovechkin won five times, Detroit's Pavel Datsyuk was named winner of the Kharlamov

Trophy for the first time in 2011. He started the 2010–11 season with a Gordie Howe Hat Trick on opening night and went on to finish with 59 points (23 goals, 36 assists) in 56 games. Two seasons later, Datsyuk won it again, having excelled in the lockout-shortened 48-game season and finishing with 49 points (15 goals, 34 assists) in 47 games.

Fedorov and Datsyuk got plenty of recognition on this side of the Atlantic as well. Each was selected to the 100 Greatest NHL Players in 2017, the league's centennial.

36 There are three players named Howe in the Hockey Hall of Fame. Two are related, none played together with the Red Wings, but all of them wore the winged wheel during their NHL careers.

Of course, Gordie Howe is the most famous. But he wasn't the first. In fact, when Gordie reported to training camp with the Red Wings, in 1946, the most common question he was asked was, "Are you related to Syd Howe?"

The answer was no, but the first Howe to wear a Detroit uniform had left an impressive set of accomplishments for Gordie to follow.

They had one other thing in common: Each held the all-time NHL lead in scoring at one point in time. Syd Howe took the all-time lead on March 8, 1945, when he had an assist in Detroit's 7–3 victory against the New York Rangers. It was the 516th point of his NHL career, moving him past Nels Stewart, who retired after the 1939–40 season with 515.

Syd added one more point to his record before the end of the 1944–45 season, and 11 more in 1945–46, finishing his NHL career with 528 points. But his time atop the points list was short. He was passed by Bill Cowley of the Boston Bruins on February 12, 1947. Eighteen years later, he was elected to the Hockey Hall of Fame.

Unlike Gordie, Syd Howe never led the NHL in any offensive category. The closest he came was finishing second, in 1934–35, with 47 points in 50 games (10 points behind Charlie Conacher). That was the season he came to Detroit in a trade with the St. Louis Eagles.

Syd Howe did have one accomplishment Gordie couldn't match: He scored six goals in a single game, on February 3, 1944, in a 12–2 victory against the New York Rangers in Detroit. It's still the most by any player since the introduction of the red line in 1943. The mark has been equaled twice—by Red Berenson in 1968 and Darryl Sittler in 1976—but never surpassed.

As Syd Howe was leaving, Gordie was arriving. The teenager from Floral, Saskatchewan, came to camp with the Wings in 1946 and kept on coming for 25 seasons, until he hung up his red jersey after the 1970–71 season. The Hockey Hall of Fame waived its mandatory three-year wait and inducted Howe a few months later.

But it turned out he wasn't ready to hang up his skates. After two seasons off, Gordie Howe joined the Houston Aeros of the World Hockey Association, partly because he would be able to play with sons Mark and Marty. The three Howes played four seasons with the Aeros and two with the New England Whalers before the WHA went under and the Whalers became one of four teams admitted to the NHL. All three returned to the NHL with the renamed Hartford Whalers for the 1979–80 season, and Gordie played all 80 games, finishing with 41 points (15 goals, 26 assists), before finally calling it a career at the age of 52.

That left Mark and Marty. But while Marty bounced between the NHL and the American Hockey League before retiring in 1985, Mark Howe's career was ready for takeoff. After surviving a scary injury with the Whalers, he was traded to the Philadelphia Flyers on August 19, 1982.

For most of the next decade, Mark Howe was among the best defensemen in the NHL. He was a three-time First-Team All-Star and Norris Trophy runner-up, had as many as 24 goals and 85 points in a season, and led the NHL with a plus-85 rating in 1985–86.

Injuries had made Mark Howe a part-time player by the early 1990s. The Flyers, who had fallen on hard times, let him become a free agent after the 1991–92 season so he could have a chance to win the Stanley Cup by signing with the Red Wings, who were on the rise.

Mark Howe became a steadying influence on a young, talented defense—most notably helping Nicklas Lidstrom get used to the NHL. He helped the Red Wings reach the Stanley Cup Final in 1995, but they were swept by the New Jersey Devils and Howe decided to retire. He joined Syd and Gordie in the Hall of Fame in 2011.

37 Gordie Howe won the Hart Trophy six times, more than anyone in NHL history whose name isn't Wayne Gretzky. But when he won the Hart for the first time in 1951–52, Mr. Hockey wasn't the first—and not even the second—member of the Red Wings to take home the trophy.

Sid Abel, Howe's center on the "Production Line," had won the Hart three years earlier. But the first Detroit player to be honored as the NHL's MVP was one of the league's most versatile players, someone who starred as a forward and later played as a defenseman.

Red Wings scouts found Ebbie Goodfellow, a slick center, playing amateur hockey in Ottawa. He was signed and sent to the Detroit Olympics of the Canadian Professional Hockey League in 1928–29, where he led the league in scoring with 26 goals and 34 points.

He joined the Red Wings in 1929–30 and scored 17 goals in his first NHL season. Goodfellow was a solid player in the middle for Detroit—he scored 25 goals in 48 games in 1930–31—but in 1934 he switched to defense at the request of coach Jack Adams.

Amazingly, he was even better as a defenseman. With Goodfellow now on the blue line, the Wings won the Stanley Cup for the first time in 1936, then repeated in 1937. Goodfellow was named to the NHL's Second All-Star Team in 1936, and twice named to the First All-Star Team, first in the 1936–37 season and again in 1939–40. He was chosen to appear in the All-Star games held in 1937 and 1939.

Goodfellow won the Hart Trophy as the NHL's most valuable player in 1939–40 and helped the Wings win the Stanley Cup again in 1943, when he became the last playing coach to guide his team to a championship. He took over after Adams was suspended during the playoffs.

Goodfellow retired after the 1943 Cup victory and was elected to the Hockey Hall of Fame in 1963. He was a founding member of the Detroit Red Wings Alumni Association, which was formed in 1959 and is still in operation today.

38 When the team we now know as the Red Wings entered the NHL, it was known as the Detroit Cougars. That's largely because the owners of the new team purchased many of its players from the Victoria Cougars of the Western Hockey League, which was in the process of going out of business. Victoria was one of the most successful teams in the WHL. The Cougars had won the Stanley Cup in 1925 (the last non-NHL team to do so) and lost in the Final in 1926.

Like many expansion teams, the new Detroit entry had some growing pains. It took three seasons for the Cougars to make their first trip to the Stanley Cup Playoffs, where they lost a two-game, total-goal series to the Toronto Maple Leafs.

In 1930, with the team still struggling, coach/general manager Jack Adams changed the team name to the Detroit Falcons. The uniforms changed as well. Gold was introduced to the color scheme, joining the red and white used by the Cougars. It was the only time in franchise history that a color other than red and white was used.

The Falcons weren't much more successful than the Cougars. They failed to qualify for the playoffs in 1930–31, then lost a two-game, total-goals series to the Montreal Maroons. Money was still tight: Adams once joked that if the Montreal Canadiens made forward Howie Morenz, one of the NHL's first superstars, available to him for $1.98, Detroit couldn't afford him.

The money problems ended in 1932, when James Norris, a grain millionaire and shipping magnate, bought the team. The new owner had once played for the Montreal Amateur Athletic Association's Winged Wheelers, and, when he met Adams, the two decided that the new logo would be a winged wheel and the team would be known as the Red Wings. The uniforms reverted to red and white, removing the gold that had accompanied the name change to the Falcons two years earlier. They've changed very little since then.

39 In the spring of 1952, hockey pucks must have looked like beach balls to Terry Sawchuk.

After another brilliant regular season, in which he went 44–14–12 with a 1.90 goals-against average and 12 shutouts, he won the Vezina

Trophy and helped the Red Wings finish first with 100 points, then an NHL record.

The Red Wings opened the Stanley Cup Playoffs at home against the defending champion Toronto Maple Leafs, and Sawchuk just kept rolling. He put up back-to-back shutouts in Games 1 and 2, winning, 3–0, in the opener and forcing a first-period goal by Johnny Wilson to stand up for a 1–0 win in the second game.

The series moved to Toronto for Game 3, and the Maple Leafs finally got a puck past Sawchuk when Joe Klukay scored at 11:16 of the first period to tie the game, 1–1. Max Bentley got another goal for Toronto at 12:20 of the second period, but by then, the Red Wings had run off three straight for a 4–1 lead. Bentley made it a two-goal game, but Detroit's Johnny Wilson and Benny Woit scored in the third period for a 6–2 win and a 3–0 lead in the series.

The Leafs took their first lead in the series when Harry Watson scored 2:56 into the first period of Game 4. But Ted Lindsay tied the game 1:39 later, and Tony Leswick put Detroit ahead to stay before the midway mark of the period. Sid Abel's goal early in the second period made it 3–1—and the way Sawchuk was playing, a two-goal lead might as well have been a 10-goal advantage.

The final tally: Four games, three goals allowed, two shutouts, and a goals-against average of 0.75.

Amazingly, that was just a warmup for Sawchuk's performance in the Stanley Cup Final against the Montreal Canadiens, who had finished second and eliminated the fourth-place Boston Bruins in seven games.

The series began at the Forum in Montreal on April 10, and Sawchuk was unbeatable for more than 51 minutes. When Montreal defenseman Tom Johnson scored at 11:01 of the third period, all he did was cut Detroit's 2–0 lead in half; Leswick had scored the game's first goal at 3:27 of the second and the second at 7:59 of the third.

The Canadiens couldn't put another puck past Sawchuk. Lindsay put the game away by scoring with 16 seconds remaining to seal a 3–1 win.

All the scoring in Game 2 on April 12 took place before the game was 21 minutes old. Detroit's Marty Pavelich and Montreal's Elmer

Lach traded goals late in the first period, and Lindsay made it 2–1 with an unassisted goal 21 seconds into the second. That was all the offense, as Sawchuk kept the Canadiens off the board and sent the Red Wings back to the Olympia with a 2–0 lead in the best-of-seven series.

The packed house that turned out for Game 3 the next night saw another Sawchuk gem. Gordie Howe scored twice and set up a goal by Lindsay in a 3–0 win that put the Wings on the verge of back-to-back sweeps.

By now, the Canadiens had to be wondering if they would ever score against Sawchuk again. The answer was simple: not in this series. Sawchuk made 26 saves, Metro Prystal scored twice and set up Glen Skov's goal, and the Wings completed a perfect postseason with another 3–0 win.

Had there been a Conn Smythe Trophy in that era (it wasn't instituted until 1965), Sawchuk would have been a shoo-in. After allowing just two goals to the Canadiens, his final ledger for the playoffs was eight games, eight wins, no losses, five goals allowed, a goals-against average of 0.63 and four shutouts. All five goals allowed came on the road, none in the four games played in Detroit. More than six decades later, it's still among the greatest goaltending performances in Stanley Cup history.

40 Beirut, Lebanon, isn't exactly a hockey hotbed. Ed Hatoum, a forward who played parts of two seasons with the Red Wings, was the first (and still only) player born in Lebanon to make it to the NHL.

Hatoum was born in Beirut on December 7, 1947. He moved to Ottawa at age 10 with his father and brother; his mom and six siblings arrived soon afterward.

"I came at the age of 10," he told the *Vancouver Province* in 2015. "I had never skated in my life, but we lived right next to the rink, and in those days during the winter, there wasn't much else to do.

"So I got a pair of old skates that didn't fit me and learned to skate, and I ended up playing four years with the Hamilton Red Wings of the OHA [Ontario Hockey Association, now the Ontario Hockey League]."

Hatoum's ancestry drew more than a few snarky remarks, but his speed and skill earned him a spot on the Fort Worth Red Wings of the Central Hockey League in 1968–69, his first pro season. He had 21 goals and 49 points in 53 games, earning a 16-game call-up from the parent club, where he had earned two goals and three points.

Hatoum got only five games with the Wings in 1969–70, though, as he recounted to the *Province*, his demotion back to the minors took one Red Wings legend by surprise.

"When they sent me back down and I was packing up, [Gordie] Howe came over and said, 'Where are you going?' I said, 'They sent me back,' and he said, 'What's going on here? We need young legs on this team.' But it was like that in those days," he said. "The big players didn't have any influence with the coaches and owners."

The Vancouver Canucks took Hatoum in the 1970 expansion draft. He played one season with the Canucks, and later spent time in the Western Hockey League and the World Hockey Association before retiring.

If nothing else, the 5-foot-10, 180-pound forward should be remembered for having one of the great hockey nicknames of all time, "Sock." Try saying "Sock Hatoum" fast, and it sounds like "Sock it to 'Em." A perfect hockey nickname.

OVERTIME

You've made it through three periods, given it all you've got. Now it's time to see how much you still have in the tank. Some real toughies are coming. Overtime awaits!

1 Steve Yzerman was the captain of the Red Wings from 1986 to 2006. Who did he replace? There's a bonus point if you know who got the "C" when "Stevie Y" called it a career. *Answer on page 195.*
   a. Danny Gare
   b. Gerard Gallant
   c. Dennis Hextall
   d. Reed Larson

2 For decades, NHL teams generally used only uniform numbers from 1 through 30. That's changed over the years, obviously, with the Red Wings using numbers as high as 96 (Tomas Holmstrom). But there are still a few numbers that haven't been used. What is the lowest number that's never been issued to a Red Wing? *Answer on page 196.*
   a. No. 45
   b. No. 54
   c. No. 65
   d. No. 76

3 Of the 90 players who have spent at least one game as a goaltender with the Red Wings since the team entered the NHL in 1926 through the end of the 2017–18 season, just one has a

191

perfect record: at least one victory, no ties, and no losses. Who is he? *Answer on page 198.*

4 The Red Wings are one of the Original Six, the half-dozen teams that made up the NHL from 1942 to 1967, so, naturally, they've played those clubs far more than any of the 30 opponents they faced in 2017–18. They have won more than 300 games against just one of those teams. Which one? *Answer on page 199.*
a. Boston Bruins
b. Chicago Blackhawks
c. New York Rangers
d. Toronto Maple Leafs

5 Who was the first Red Wings coach to win the Jack Adams Award as the NHL's top coach? *Answer on page 200.*
a. Sid Abel
b. Scotty Bowman
c. Alex Delvecchio
d. Bobby Kromm

6 The arrival of the shootout in 2005 meant that NHL games would no longer end in a tie. Who was the Red Wings' opponent in their last tie, and when was it played? *Answers on page 202.*

7 Three players share the Red Wings' record for most career assists by a goaltender. Which of these players is *not* one of the three? *Answer on page 204.*
a. Tim Cheveldae
b. Chris Osgood
c. Terry Sawchuk
d. Greg Stefan

8 Only one Red Wings player has scored goals in each of the first six games of a season. Who did it? *Answer on page 205.*

a. Brett Hull
b. Gordie Howe
c. Ted Lindsay
d. Steve Yzerman

9 Several Red Wings have scored three goals in a period. Henrik Zetterberg was the last to do so, on January 18, 2015, against the Buffalo Sabres. Four Detroit players have scored three power-play goals in a game. But who is the only one to score three power-play goals in the same period? *Answer on page 207.*
a. Jimmy Carson
b. Gordie Howe
c. Mickey Redmond
d. Steve Yzerman

10 No Red Wing has worn No. 9 since Gordie Howe, who retired after the 1970–71 and had his number officially retired on March 12, 1972. But 20 players wore No. 9 before Mr. Hockey. Who was the last one? Hint, when he was traded, Howe switched numbers and took No. 9. *Answer on page 208.*
a. Sid Abel
b. Mud Bruneteau
c. Roy Conacher
d. Bill Thompson

OVERTIME

1 Steve Yzerman wasn't named captain of the Red Wings when he showed up as a rookie in 1983, though it might have seemed that way.

When Yzerman was drafted in 1983, Danny Gare had completed his first season as Detroit's captain, after succeeding defenseman Reed Larson. Gare had been a 50-goal scorer twice with the Buffalo Sabres before the Red Wings acquired him in a six-player trade on December 2, 1981.

Unfortunately for the Wings, Gare's biggest scoring seasons were behind him. He dropped from 46 goals with the Sabres in 1980–81 to 20 in 1981–82, though 13 of those 20 came in 36 games with the Red Wings after the trade. That was enough to convince the Wings to name Gare as their new captain, which they did prior to the 1982–83 season.

Gare was wearing the "C" when Yzerman arrived after being taken with the No. 4 selection in the 1983 NHL Draft, and he continued to serve as captain through 1985–86. When the Red Wings opted to let Gare leave as a free agent (he signed with the Edmonton Oilers and played 18 games before retiring), coach Jacques Demers decided that even though Yzerman was just 21 years old, he should get the captaincy.

No one could have known that Yzerman would never skate another NHL game without a "C" on his sweater.

Yzerman spent the next 20 years, until his retirement in 2006, as Detroit's captain. He received the Stanley Cup from NHL Commissioner Gary Bettman after the Red Wings ended their 42-year championship drought in 1997, and again in 1998 and 2002.

One of Yzerman's regular linemates was Gerard Gallant, who had 39 goals, 93 points, and 230 penalty minutes with Yzerman as his center in 1988–89. Gallant was an alternate captain during his time in Detroit, and he wore the "C" while Yzerman was injured late in the 1988–89 season.

But all good things must come to an end, and that included Yzerman's NHL career. Yzerman hung up his skates after the 2005–06 season and was elected to the Hockey Hall of Fame in 2009, the first year he was eligible, after having turned over the captaincy to defenseman Nicklas Lidstrom. Lidstrom kept it for six seasons, until he retired in 2012, joining Yzerman in the Hall of Fame three years later.

2 As much as some fans might long for the days when all NHL players wore numbers from 1 to 30, the facts are that numbers today go all the way to No. 98; No. 99 has been retired around the NHL in honor of Wayne Gretzky.

Of course, not nearly as many players have worn numbers above 30, and as the numbers get higher, some have been worn rarely, if at all. Though every number from 00 to 99 has been worn by someone in the NHL, not all of them have been worn by a member of the Red Wings.

No Detroit player had worn No. 45 until the 2005–06 season, when it was issued to defenseman Kyle Quincey, the Red Wings' fourth-round pick (No. 132) in the 2003 NHL Draft. Quincey wore it for one game that season after being recalled from the Grand Rapids Griffins of the American Hockey League.

Quincey bounced back and forth between the Wings and Grand Rapids for the next two seasons, and when he played six games for Detroit in 2007–08, he did it while wearing No. 4. The Red Wings lost him on waivers to the Los Angeles Kings in October of 2008. The Kings sent him to the Colorado Avalanche on July 3, 2009, and he returned to the Red Wings in a trade on February 21, 2012. He wore No. 27 with the Red Wings through the 2015–16 season.

No. 65 had never been worn by a Red Wing until they signed college free agent defenseman Danny DeKeyser on March 29, 2013. DeKeyser, a native of Macomb, Michigan, had drawn attention from several NHL teams after playing three seasons at Western Michigan

Defenseman Kyle Quincey, who also wore No. 45, is one of two players in Red Wings history whose last name started with the letter "Q." (Muéro at English Wikipedia; License: CC0, via Wikimedia Commons; Source: https://commons.wikimedia.org/w/index.php?curid=24647650)

University. He's worn that number throughout his time with the Detroit and has played more than 350 games with the Red Wings.

No Detroit player had worn No. 76 until Swedish forward Fabian Brunnstrom joined the Red Wings for the 2011–12 season. Brunnstrom had been the object of a bidding war in 2008 before signing with the Dallas Stars. He had a hat trick in his first NHL game, against the Nashville Predators on October 15, 2009, and finished the season with 29 points (17 goals, 12 assists) in 59 games. But he had just 11 points (two goals, nine assists) in 2009–10 and ended the season in the minors.

The Red Wings signed Brunnstrom as a free agent on July 26, 2011. After spending a season with Grand Rapids in the AHL, his debut with Detroit was further delayed by the lockout that shortened the 2012–13 season to 48 games. He made the Red Wings after training camp but played only five games and had one assist. Brunnstrom wound up back in Sweden and spent the rest of his career in Europe.

As for No. 54? It's still waiting for the first Red Wing to wear it.

3 Terry Sawchuk and Chris Osgood each won more than 300 games wearing the winged wheel, but they were far from perfect during their time with Detroit. Through the 2017–18 season, 67 goaltenders have won at least one game—but only one has a victory without a tie or overtime loss.

Ladies and gentlemen, meet Tom McCollum.

The Red Wings actually had big plans for McCollum after they made him the last player (No. 30) picked in the first round of the 2008 NHL Draft. It came after he went 25–17–6 with a 2.50 goals-against average in his second season with the Guelph Storm of the Ontario Hockey League. Though the Red Wings were coming off their fourth Stanley Cup championship in 12 seasons, goaltenders Dominik Hasek and Osgood each were on the far side of 30, so the hope was that McCollum could grow into the No. 1 job.

McCollum went back to junior hockey in 2008–09, splitting the season between Guelph and the Brampton Battalion, finishing with a 34–16–4 record and going 13–8 in the playoffs for Brampton.

That was McCollum's last season in juniors. He spent most of the 2010–11 season with Grand Rapids, the Red Wings' farm team in the American Hockey League, but made his NHL debut on March 30, 2011, when he relieved Joey MacDonald in the second period of what turned out to be a 10–3 loss to the St. Louis Blues. McCollum entered the game at 5:23 of the second period and allowed three goals on eight shots. MacDonald returned to the game and played the third period.

Then it was back to the minors. McCollum spent most of the next three seasons in Grand Rapids, with a couple of stints at Toledo of the ECHL. He helped Grand Rapids win the Calder Cup championship in 2013 and was playing for the Griffins in 2014–15 when injuries left the Red Wings short in goal and McCollum got his second call-up.

McCollum made his second NHL appearance on January 18, 2015. Again he came on in relief, this time after Petr Mrazek allowed three goals on seven shots in the first 13:37 against the Buffalo Sabres at Joe Louis Arena. The Red Wings tied the game with three goals in the second period, then scored three more in the third. McCollum allowed one goal on eight shots and got credit for the 6–4 victory.

McCollum made one more appearance, stopping all 17 shots he faced in relief during the third period of a 5–1 road loss to the Tampa Bay Lightning 11 days later. Soon after, he was returned to Grand Rapids, never to play for Detroit again.

McCollum remained in the Red Wings' system through the 2015–16 season, then signed with the Calgary Flames on October 15, 2016. He spent the 2016–17 season with three minor-league teams before being reacquired by the Red Wings on July 1, 2017. McCollum went 20–14–2 with a 2.64 goals-against average and a .912 save percentage with Grand Rapids in 2017–18.

McCollum signed with Milwaukee, the AHL affiliate of the Nashville Predators, on July 17, 2018, meaning that his status as the only goaltender in Red Wings history to have at least one victory with no losses or ties could last a while.

4 The Red Wings and Chicago Blackhawks, originally known as the Black Hawks, entered the NHL together as part of the league's expansion in 1926, and the Wings have largely had their way with the Hawks during their nine-plus decades together on the ice.

Entering the 2018–19 season, the teams had played 735 times in the regular season, with Detroit winning 368, losing 269 in regulation, eight in overtime, and six in shootouts, and tying 84 times. They are 219–108 with 33 ties and six overtime/shootout losses in home games and 150–161 with 51 ties and eight OT/SO losses in road games. In the 1950s, the Black Hawks were the home team in six games against the Red Wings that were played in Indianapolis, St. Louis, and Omaha, and Detroit was 5–0–1 in those games.

Detroit's domination of its Midwest rival really took off after World War II, when the Red Wings became one of the NHL's elite teams and the Hawks hit the skids. The Wings won 11 in a row against Chicago from March 2, 1947 (3–1 at Chicago Stadium) through January 1, 1948 (4–1 at Chicago).

The Wings ran off 12 straight wins against the Hawks from December 19, 1950 (6–1 at the Olympia) through November 15, 1951 (3–1 at Detroit). They also went 18–1–1 in a stretch of 20 games from January 30, 1954 (4–2 at Detroit) through March 12, 1955 (3–2 at the Olympia).

The Black Hawks began to come out of their tailspin in the late 1950s and started to have more success against the Red Wings. They were 13–1–2 during a 16-game stretch from October 28, 1965 (5–1 at Detroit) through October 23, 1966 (4–1 at Chicago), and went 14–0–1 from October 15, 1970 (2–1 at Detroit) through January 17, 1973 (6–4 at Detroit).

Detroit had a pair of seven-game winning streaks in the 2000s. The Blackhawks won seven in a row from February 21, 2012 (2–1 at Chicago) through April 12, 2013 (3–2 at Chicago). However, four of the seven wins came past regulation, meaning the Red Wings got a point.

The Red Wings' most recent shutout (through the 2017–18 season) came on January 14, 2018, when they won 4–0 at Chicago. The Blackhawks haven't shut out the Wings since winning 3–0 at Joe Louis Arena on December 23, 2009.

5 The NHL instituted the Jack Adams Award in the 1973–74 season to honor its Coach of the Year, meaning that it came along too early for Sid Abel. The longtime Wings star took over behind the bench midway through the 1957–58 season and stayed there through 1969–70. The Red Wings made the Stanley Cup Playoffs eight times under Abel, and advanced to the Final in four of those seasons but were never able to bring home a championship.

Had the Jack Adams been around in 1964–65, Abel might well have won it. The Red Wings finished first that season by going 40–23–7, though they were upset in the Semifinals.

Scotty Bowman has more wins (1,244) in the regular season than any coach in NHL history, but perhaps amazingly, he won the Jack Adams just twice. The first time was in 1976–77 with the Montreal Canadiens, who had set NHL single-season records for wins (60) and points (132) in an 80-game season. The second came with the 1995–96 Red Wings, who broke that record for victories by winning 62 games and finishing with 131 points in an 82-game season.

Alex Delvecchio was a Hall of Famer and one of the greatest players in Wings history. He took over for Abel as center on the famed "Production Line" and played his entire career with Detroit until retiring in 1973. The Red Wings wasted no time putting Delvecchio behind the bench, but he was much less successful as a coach than he'd been as a player. Delvecchio coached parts of four seasons with the

Hall of Famer Alex Delvecchio was honored with his own statue by the Red Wings. (Kevin Ward—https://www.flickr.com/photos/kw111786/3183526997/; License: CC by -SA 2.0; Source: https://commons.wikimedia.org/w/index.php?curid=28832211)

Red Wings, going 82–131–32 and failing to get them into the Stanley Cup Playoffs.

Bobby Kromm came to the Wings in 1977 after two spectacularly successful seasons with the Winnipeg Jets of the World Hockey Association that included an Avco Cup (the WHA's version of the Stanley Cup) in 1976. He took a team that hadn't made the playoffs since Abel's last season in 1969–70 and led the Wings to the postseason with a 32–34–14 record and 78 points, a 37-point improvement from 1976–77. They scored 69 more goals and reduced their goals-allowed by 42. Detroit swept its best-of-three Preliminary Round series against the Atlanta Flames before losing to the Canadiens in five games in the Quarterfinals. The improvement earned Kromm the Jack Adams Award, the first Red Wings coach to be honored as the NHL's best.

But the Red Wings struggled under Kromm in 1978–79, and he was fired late in the 1979–80 season. Kromm never coached in the NHL again, though his son, Richard Kromm, spent 10 seasons as a player with the Calgary Flames and New York Islanders. His record with Detroit was 79–111–41. He died in 2010 at age 82.

"I've been on teams that were better or equally as good that just didn't win," forward Paul Woods told Mlive.com. "It [the 1977–78 club] was a team that came together. That's what a coach can do.

"They should have kept him; we could have turned it around."

Ted Lindsay, the general manager who hired Kromm, said he did so because of his success in the World Hockey Association.

"Bobby and I were supposed to bring aggressive hockey back to the Motor City," Lindsay told Mlive.com. "He was the coach of the year and I was the [general] manager of the year, and then three years later they fired us.

"He was a no-nonsense coach," Lindsay said. "All he wanted was your best effort."

6 Yes, once upon a time (actually until 2005), NHL games that were tied after overtime (or after the regulation 60 minutes from 1942 to 1983), ended that way. No shootouts. Just one point for each team and on to the next game.

In all, the Red Wings played 815 ties from 1926 through the end of the 2003–04 season. After the lockout that wiped out the 2004–05 season, the new-look NHL resumed play using the penalty-shot competition to decide games that were tied after 65 minutes.

The Red Wings finished the 2003–04 season with 11 ties. (They also lost two other games in overtime but earned a point.) The 11th tie of the season—and ultimately the last one in Red Wings history—came when the Phoenix (now Arizona) Coyotes hosted Detroit at Glendale Arena and each team left with a point after a 1–1 tie.

Neither team scored in the first period, but the Red Wings grabbed a 1–0 lead at 11:40 of the second when Brendan Shanahan scored his 24th goal of the season, putting the puck in the net from just inside the right circle after Henrik Zetterberg won a faceoff. It was Shanahan's 557th NHL goal, moving him into 17th place on the NHL's all-time list.

The Red Wings dominated play throughout the third period, outshooting the Coyotes, 20–7. But the Coyotes got their lone goal when rookie center Erik Westrum, playing in just his seventh NHL game, scored the only goal of his NHL career by beating Curtis Joseph at 2:11. Joseph made a sprawling save of Fredrik Sjostrom's initial shot and dived to poke the puck away from the top of the crease, but Westrum took the puck off the goalie's outstretched stick, stepped to the right and put a shot into the wide-open net.

Detroit spent the rest of the period unsuccessfully trying to get the go-ahead goal past Brian Boucher, who stopped all 20 shots. He got a break when Shanahan's shot with two-tenths of a second remaining bounced past Boucher off Mathieu Schneider's skates, but referee Mike Leggo had blown his whistle just before the puck went into the net.

Boucher also survived a power play after Jeff Taffe of the Coyotes was penalized with 6:09 left in regulation. Boucher made three saves and three other shots barely missed the net. He even played 10 seconds without his stick after it was knocked behind him while he was sprawled on the ice.

The point moved the Red Wings four points ahead of the Colorado Avalanche in the Western Conference standings. It also extended

Phoenix's winless streak to 14 games, but it allowed the Coyotes to finish the season series with Detroit 1–1–2.

Coincidentally, the last tie at Joe Louis Arena was also a 1–1 game. Tomas Holmstrom's second-period goal gave the Red Wings a 1–0 lead against the Tampa Bay Lightning, but Fredrik Modin beat Manny Legace with 6:21 remaining in regulation time and neither team scored again.

7 If you were a goaltender who wanted to pile up some points, playing after the 1967 expansion that doubled the size of the NHL from six to 12 teams (on the way to 31 in 2017–18 and 32 in a couple of years) was the thing to do.

Three goaltenders in the first post-expansion era share the Red Wings record for assists during a career at 15. All three began their time with the Wings after 1980.

Greg Stefan was the first, joining the Red Wings for two games during the 1981–82 season. He played 35 games in 1982–83 without getting an assist, then began a seven-year scoring streak by getting three assists during 1983–84, when he went 19–22–2 in 50 games. After picking up two assists in each of the next two seasons, Stefan had a career-high four in 1986–87, when he was 20–17–3 in 43 appearances, and he had at least one assist in each of his final three seasons with Detroit to finish with 15.

Tim Cheveldae overlapped briefly with Stefan. His first NHL appearances (two games, both losses) came in 1988–89, and he played 28 games in 1989–90, Stefan's final season with the Wings (and in the NHL). Cheveldae had one assist in those 28 games, then piled up 13 in the next three seasons, five coming in 1990–91, four in each of the next two. Assist number 15 came before he was traded to the Winnipeg Jets on March 8, 1994. Cheveldae played in the NHL through the 1996–97 season but had only one more assist.

One reason the Red Wings felt they could trade Cheveldae was the arrival of Chris Osgood, who took the starting job in 1993–94 and went 23–8–5 with a 2.86 goals-against average. Osgood had nine assists with the Red Wings before being lost to the New York Islanders in the waiver draft before the 2001–02 season. Osgood had a career-high four assists with the Islanders that first season with them, but he didn't have another in the NHL until returning to the Red Wings during the 2005–06 season. He then had seven more assists with Detroit, including three in 2007–08. He retired after the 2010–11 with 19, all but four of which came with the Red Wings.

None of those three goaltenders came close to the 734 games played with Detroit by Hall of Famer Terry Sawchuk, but Sawchuk managed just three assists with the Wings and seven in his career. With Detroit, he had one each in 1953–54, 1954–55, and 1960–61.

8 Brett Hull, Gordie Howe, and Ted Lindsay are all in the Hockey Hall of Fame, but none of them could do what another Hall of Famer, Steve Yzerman, did in 1988–89: score goals in each of the first six games of a season.

Yzerman was already an established star who was coming off a 50-goal, 102-point season, each an NHL career high, when 1988–89 began. So it wasn't a surprise when he scored Detroit's first goal of the new season, a power-play tally 5:22 into the opener against the Los Angeles Kings at the Forum in Inglewood, California, on October 6.

Unfortunately for Yzerman and the Wings, that was about the last thing that went right that night. Wayne Gretzky, making his debut with the Kings two months after being acquired from the Edmonton Oilers, tied the game at 12:54 and assisted on three goals in what turned into an 8–2 rout.

Yzerman, who was born in Cranbrook, British Columbia, made it two goals in two games two nights later, when the Red Wings continued their road trip against the Vancouver Canucks at Pacific Coliseum. This time, the results were better for Yzerman and his teammates. His goal at 11:52 of the third period cut Vancouver's lead to 3–2, and he had the primary assist when Dave Barr scored at 16:08 to give the Red Wings a 3–3 tie and a point.

The trip continued two nights later against the Calgary Flames (who went on to win the Stanley Cup), and so did Yzerman's streak. Yzerman scored a power-play goal at 13:50 of the first period that tied the game, 1–1. Paul MacLean scored to put the Red Wings ahead, 2–1, after one period, but Calgary scored four unanswered goals in the second period and cruised to a 5–2 win.

The Red Wings headed home with an 0–2–1 record to play the St. Louis Blues at Joe Louis Arena on October 14—and the teams played the wildest home opener in NHL history.

Detroit appeared to have a comfortable 7–3 lead after two periods, with Yzerman scoring one of Detroit's four goals in the second. But the Blues scored five times in the third period, before MacLean's goal with 30 seconds remaining tied the game, 8–8. Each team left with a point after the scoreless overtime, and Yzerman's goal-scoring streak was now four games.

The Wings jumped right on a plane for the short trip to Toronto and a game the next night at Maple Leaf Gardens. This time it was the Red Wings' turn to overcome a third-period deficit. They trailed, 3–1, after Dave Reid scored for Toronto at 2:08, but the rest of the period belonged to Detroit. Yzerman set up Adam Graves's goal at 5:30, Miroslav Frycer tied it 27 seconds later, Barr put the Red Wings ahead at 8:30, and Yzerman's goal with 30 seconds remaining sealed the 5–3 win.

Back at home against the Chicago Blackhawks on October 18, Yzerman used every possible second to extend his streak to six games. The Hawks led, 3–0, after Duane Sutter scored at 11:27 of the second period. But Shane Burr started Detroit's comeback when he scored 25 seconds later. Lee Norwood cut the margin to 3–2 at 17:45 of the third period, and MacLean's goal 45 seconds later sent the game to overtime.

Time was running out on Yzerman's streak when he broke in and scored at 4:59 of overtime to give the Red Wings a thrilling 4–3 win (spoiling the NHL debut of another future Hall of Famer, Ed Belfour in the process). The goal streak did come to an end three nights later, when Yzerman was limited to an assist, as the Maple Leafs got some revenge with a 4–2 win at Joe Louis Arena.

Yzerman couldn't keep up the goal-a-game pace, but he did go on to have his best offensive season with 65 goals and 155 points, totals no Detroit player has approached since.

9 The NHL in the late 1980s and early 1990s was vastly different than the game in the 21st century. Though the pace of the game was much slower than today, there were a lot more goals scored, usually more than seven per game. (The average since 2005–06 is about 5.5.)

One reason there were more goals was the abundance of power plays, when it wasn't unusual to see a team receive seven opportunities or more. Combine that with the presence of some of the great scorers in NHL history—Wayne Gretzky, Mario Lemieux, and Detroit's Steve Yzerman—and you wind up with a high-scoring era.

With lots of goals on an average night, especially power-play goals, teams scoring three man-advantage goals in a period wasn't unusual. But even in that high-scoring era, getting three on the power play was unique.

Fans at Maple Leaf Gardens probably came back from the second intermission of their December 27, 1989, game feeling pretty good. Toronto had scored five goals in the second period and took a 7–3 lead into the final 20 minutes against the Red Wings.

But Toronto defenseman Tom Kurvers had taken a hooking penalty with three seconds left in the second period, negating the final 10 seconds of a Maple Leafs power play. Steve Yzerman jumped onto the ice after his penalty expired, and Jimmy Carson made the Maple Leafs pay when he scored at 53 seconds to make it 7–4.

There were some rumbles when Yzerman scored at 2:24 to make it 7–5: Could the Leafs really blow a four-goal lead in the third period? The answer turned out to be yes, because Toronto couldn't stop filling the penalty box.

The teams were already playing four-on-four when Toronto's Wendel Clark was called for interference at 9:53, and things got worse when John McIntyre went off for high sticking at 11:18.

With the Red Wings playing five-on-three, Carson scored again at 11:44 to make it 7–6. Detroit still had a five-on-four power play because of McIntyre's penalty, and it took Carson just 30 seconds to complete his power-play hat trick in the third period and tie the game, 7–7.

The Red Wings had two more power-play chances and the Maple

Leafs got one, but neither team was able to score again, and the game ended, 7–7. Carson joined Ted Lindsay (March 20, 1955) as the only Red Wings to score three times in one period. Zetterberg (February 17, 2007) and Tomas Holmstrom (February 24, 2007), joined them, but Carson is the only one to get all three of his on the power play.

10 If you've come this far, you know that Gordie Howe didn't wear No. 9 when he began his career with the Red Wings.

In fact, No. 9 was one of those numbers that got passed around a lot. The only Red Wing to wear it for more than three straight seasons was Mud Bruneteau, who wore it from 1937–38 through 1945–46, but he didn't have it exclusively. No less than eight other players wore No. 9 for at least one game during that stretch. The most famous was Sid Abel, who wore it briefly in 1945–46.

Abel actually spent most of his time in Detroit wearing No. 12, which the Red Wings retired on April 29, 1995. He went back to his usual No. 12 after the 1945–46 season, and that opened up No. 9 for forward Roy Conacher, who was acquired from the Boston Bruins for Joe Carveth in August 1946.

Conacher had scored 26 goals as a rookie in 1938–39, and he had 24 each in 1940–41 and 1941–42 before heading off to fight in World War II. He missed nearly four full seasons while serving in Canada's military, then picked up where he left off. In fact, he had a career-high 30 goals for the Red Wings in 1946–47, finishing second in the NHL to the 45 scored by Maurice Richard of the Montreal Canadiens. He ended up seventh in the NHL with 54 points.

That same season, the Red Wings finished 22–27–11, fourth in the six-team NHL, and were eliminated in five games by the Toronto Maple Leafs in the Semifinals. General manager Jack Adams wasn't happy and decided moves had to be made.

On October 22, 1947, the Red Wings traded Conacher to the New York Rangers for forward Ed Slowinski and future considerations. But Conacher refused to report to New York, and the trade was voided.

Nine days later (and with Adams no doubt steaming by now), Conacher was sold to the Chicago Black Hawks. Conacher continued to excel with the struggling Hawks, scoring at least 22 goals in each of the next five seasons and winning the Art Ross Trophy as the NHL's scoring champion in 1948–49. He retired after playing 12 games in 1951–52 and was inducted into the Hockey Hall of Fame in 1998.

Conacher's departure freed up No. 9, which Howe wore until 1970–71. It was retired on March 12, 1972.

Okay, you've made it through OT. But you're not done yet. Time to dig down deep for those last few questions. On to the shootout!

You've battled your way to the end without flinching. And you've probably learned a few things about your favorite team you might not have known. Now it's time for the toughest, most challenging questions. Let's get to the shootout!

1 The NHL draft was known as the amateur draft when it began in 1963. The Red Wings, picking second, selected the only player chosen in the first two rounds who went on to become an NHL All-Star. He and his more famous brother played together in Detroit for one season and were teammates for several seasons with another NHL team. He came back to Detroit and finished his NHL career with the Wings. Who is he? *Answer on page 213.*

2 The Red Wings played 1,456 regular-season games at Joe Louis Arena before moving into Little Caesars Arena at the beginning of the 2017–18 season. They had a winning record there against all but one of 24 teams that played there at least 35 times. Which visiting team was the only one to win more games than it lost at "The Joe?" *Answer on page 214.*
a. Boston Bruins
b. Chicago Blackhawks
c. Montreal Canadiens
d. New York Rangers

3 In a way, the Red Wings were lucky to get Gordie Howe. As a teenager growing up in Saskatchewan, Howe initially drew the interest of another NHL team, but that team ultimately

decided not to sign him. Which team made this decision it would undoubtedly want to have back? *Answer on page 215.*
a. Boston Bruins
b. Chicago Black Hawks
c. New York Rangers
d. Toronto Maple Leafs

4   In addition to the numbers hanging from the rafters at Little Caesars Arena, you'll never see a Red Wing wearing No. 6. Why not? *Answer on page 216.*

5   For all their greatness, Gordie Howe and Nicklas Lidstrom were part of "only" four Stanley Cup winning teams with the Red Wings. Just one man can claim to have been part of the Wings through eight championship seasons during his six-plus decades with the team. Who was he? *Answer on page 218.*

You've made it! The final horn has sounded and your biggest test is over. Check your answers and see how you've done. Hopefully you've had some fun and maybe learned a few things about the Red Wings along the way.

SHOOTOUT

1 By the early 1960s, the NHL wanted to phase out the sponsorship of junior teams by its six clubs. NHL teams sponsored amateur teams and players, preempting other NHL clubs from acquiring new talent and limiting amateur players' hopes of making it in the NHL to the team that sponsored them.

League president Clarence Campbell wanted to move toward what he called "a uniform opportunity for each team to acquire a star player." With that in mind, the NHL held its first amateur draft on June 5, 1963, at the Queen Elizabeth Hotel in Montreal.

It wasn't like today's draft, which includes players from around the world, some of whom are already playing professional hockey. Eligibility for this draft was limited to amateur players who would reach 17 years of age between August 1, 1963, and July 31, 1964, and teams were not permitted to talk to the drafted players about turning pro until they turned 18. At that point, the teams had 72 hours to get the players signed or placed on their negotiation list. Players already on sponsorship lists were ineligible. That meant few top prospects would be available during the four rounds, because most of the top junior players were already controlled by NHL clubs through their junior teams.

The Montreal Canadiens wound up with the first pick and selected Garry Monahan, a center from the St. Michael's Buzzers of the Metro Junior B League in Toronto. Monahan went on to play 748 NHL games with five teams, including the Red Wings.

Detroit had the second pick and selected a teammate of Monahan, Peter Mahovlich, a huge right wing whose older brother, Frank, was a star with the Toronto Maple Leafs. Peter finished his junior career with the Hamilton Red Wings of the Ontario Hockey Association (now the Ontario Hockey League) and made his debut with Detroit in 1966, earning one assist in three games. For the next three seasons, he bounced between the Red Wings and their top minor-league team.

Peter, nicknamed "The Little M," got to play with Frank, known as "The Big M" (although "The Bigger M" would have been a more appropriate name for the 6-foot-5, 215-pound younger brother) after a blockbuster trade brought Frank to Detroit on March 3, 1968. They were teammates for the 30 games that Peter spent with the Red Wings during the 1968–69 season.

The Red Wings traded Peter to the Canadiens on June 6, 1969. Now 23, he split the 1969–70 season between the Canadiens and the Montreal Voyageurs of the American Hockey League.

"The Little M" had a breakout season in 1970–71. He scored 35 goals and finished with 61 points, then helped the Canadiens to a surprising Stanley Cup championship. By that time, he and Frank had been reunited, after a late-season deal brought the older Mahovlich to Montreal.

Peter turned into a star in Montreal, scoring 34 or more goals five time in a span of six seasons and putting up 117 points in 1974–75 and 105 points in 1975–76, when the Canadiens won the first of four straight Stanley Cup championships.

The Canadiens traded Peter Mahovlich to the Pittsburgh Penguins early in the 1977–78 season, and the Red Wings acquired him again on August 3, 1979. He had 16 goals and 66 points for the Red Wings in 1979–80, then played his final 24 NHL games for the Penguins in 1980–81. He finished his NHL career with 288 goals and 773 points in 884 NHL games.

2 From the Red Wings' first game at Joe Louis Arena on December 27, 1979, to their last night on April 9, 2017, they generally made life miserable for visiting teams. The Red Wings finished with a record of 828–432 with 119 ties and 77 overtime or shootout losses at "The Joe."

In all, 24 opponents played at least 35 games against the Red Wings at Joe Louis Arena. The only one to finish with a winning record was the Boston Bruins, who played exactly 40 games there and finished 20–15 with three ties and two overtime/shootout losses.

The Bruins won their first visit to the then-new Joe Louis Arena, defeating the Red Wings, 5–3, on March 5, 1980. The Bruins' next three visits all ended in ties, 4–4 on November 11, 1980, 3–3 on January 13, 1981, and 2–2 on October 22, 1981.

For the next four years, part of one of the weakest eras in Red Wings history, the Bruins made themselves right at home when they came to Detroit. Boston won six games in a row, each by at least two goals. The low point for the Red Wings came in the sixth game, a 9–2 loss on October 12, 1985.

After that, things began to get better. Detroit ended the Bruins' winning streak at Joe Louis Arena on their next visit, winning, 6–5, in overtime on January 22, 1986. The Red Wings won again, 3–1, on March 17, 1986, and went on to take four of five games against Boston.

The Bruins then won four in a row, but the Red Wings began their own four-game winning streak with a 6–1 victory on December 18, 1992.

Detroit's longest winning streak against the Bruins at The Joe was five consecutive victories, from November 3, 2009 (2–0) to October 9, 2014 (2–1). Boston won each of the next three games by the same score, 3–2, with one win each in regulation, overtime, and a shootout. The Red Wings won two of the last three, including a 6–5 shootout victory on January 18, 2017, with Frans Nielsen scoring the game-deciding goal.

3 It's hard to believe an NHL team could look at Gordie Howe, even at age 15, and not see that he could become at least a regular player, if not a star (though the latter would be asking a lot). But such was the case when the New York Rangers invited Howe to a tryout in Winnipeg in 1943. With many players in the military in World War II, NHL teams were scouring every possible source for talent, and a promising 15 year old was very much of interest.

Howe was born in Floral, Saskatchewan, and raised in Saskatoon. He said years later that the trip to Winnipeg was the first time he'd ever traveled outside the area where he'd grown up. His family was poor, and he never owned a full set of hockey equipment. As at least one story goes, he had to sit and watch other players at camp put on their equipment so he could follow their example.

Howe was homesick and returned home without a "C" form, the junior contract that would have bound him to the Rangers. One year later, Red Wings scout Fred Pinkney noticed Howe and signed him.

The Rangers have a different story, citing a 1980 article in *The New York Times* in which Howe said the Rangers did ask him to join their junior team in Regina, Saskatchewan. But Howe said he would only sign if some friends from Saskatoon would be there too. The Rangers were not interested in other kids from Howe's hometown, and he opted not to sign.

When the Red Wings wanted to sign him a year later, they assured Howe that some of his friends from Saskatchewan would be coming as well. By October 1946, Gordie was a Red Wing and on his way to becoming an NHL immortal.

Ironically, the Rangers did sign a Howe: Gordie's younger brother Vic. He played 33 games for New York between 1950 and 1955, finishing with three goals and four assists.

4 You'd have to have watched the Red Wings for a long time to have seen a player with the winged wheel on the front of his jersey and No. 6 on the back. No Red Wing has worn No. 6 since Cumming "Cummy" Burton did from 1957–59.

Burton wore No. 6 in honor of his cousin, Larry Aurie, who'd spent his entire NHL career with the Detroit Cougars/Falcons/Red Wings from 1926–27 through the end of the 1938–39 season, his last in the NHL. Burton had received special permission to do so while with the Red Wings, because the number had been retired by team owner James Norris.

At 5-foot-6, Aurie was short, even for his era. But his dedication to fitness, combined with his lack of size, earned him the nicknames "Little Dempsey" (for his fistic abilities—Jack Dempsey was a famous heavyweight boxing champion) and "The Little Rag Man" (for his entertaining ability to control or "rag" the puck while he was killing penalties).

Aurie was part of the Red Wings' first big line, playing right wing with center Marty Barry and left wing Herbie Lewis. He led the Red Wings in assists twice and topped Detroit in scoring in 1933–34 with 35 points. His highest-scoring season came in 1934–35, when he had 46 points, and he led the NHL in goals two seasons later with 23. Aurie and Lewis represented the Red Wings at the first NHL All-Star Game, a benefit game for Ace Bailey in 1934, and Aurie was a key member of the Red Wings' first Stanley Cup-winning team in 1936.

Aurie scored his 23rd goal of the 1936–37 season on March 11, 1937, in a 4–2 win against the New York Rangers. But he fractured his ankle later in the game, ending his season. Aurie was voted a First-Team All-Star, but he was never the same after the injury. After dropping to 10 goals and 19 points in 1937–38, ownership decided after the season to honor him by retiring his No. 6—the first Red Wing to be so honored.

Aurie then became player-coach of the Pittsburgh Hornets, the Red Wings' top farm team in the American Hockey League. He played one more NHL game, on January 10, 1939, and scored his last NHL goal in a 3–0 victory against the Montreal Canadiens at the Olympia.

After Burton's brief time wearing No. 6, the jersey was displayed in the lobby of the Olympia during the 1960s. However, the number was not raised to the rafters, because it wasn't customary to do so. Gordie Howe's No. 9 was retired in 1972 by then-owner Bruce Norris, but as was the case with Aurie's jersey, it, too, wasn't hung.

Aurie died on December 11, 1952, at age 47. Soon after, an article appeared in the *Red Wing Hockey Magazine*, the team's game program at the time, that eulogized Aurie and owner James Norris, who had died a week earlier:

> It was, perhaps, merciful that Mr. Norris was spared the sudden, shocking, and untimely passing of Larry Aurie.
> Larry was one of Mr. Norris' favorite players. That was man-ifested when Aurie's jersey, bearing No. 6, was retired from the

active numbers, when Larry left the Red Wing lineup for the last time.

After Mike Ilitch bought the Red Wings, in 1982, he declined to display Aurie's No. 6 along with the other retired numbers.

Red Wings vice president Jimmy Devellano told the *Detroit Free Press* in 1997 that the team refused to hang the number because Aurie was not a member of the Hockey Hall of Fame, even though No. 6 had been retired before Ilitch became owner. Thus, No. 6 has not been issued in nearly 60 years, but it's not officially retired.

5 He never played a single game for the Red Wings, but no one was part of more championship teams in Detroit than Budd Lynch, whose voice became to Wings fans what Ernie Harwell's dulcet tones were to Tigers fans.

Lynch was born in Windsor, began his broadcasting career in 1936, but put it on hold three years later top serve in the Canadian Army's Essex Scottish regiment. He was part of the force that landed on the beaches of Normandy, France, on D-Day, June 6, 1944. One month later, he lost his right arm and shoulder after being hit by a German shell in France.

Lynch returned home and resumed his radio career on CKLW in Windsor as the play-by-play voice of the Spitfires. In 1949, general manager Jack Adams hired him as the TV play-by-play man—just in time for the Red Wings to win the Stanley Cup four times in six seasons.

In 1960, Lynch became the team's radio voice for the next 15 years. He tried to retire in 1975 but ended up joining the public relations department at the behest of general manager Alex Delvecchio. Lynch wanted to retire again in the mid-1980s, but the Ilitch family persuaded him to stay with the team as the public address announcer at Joe Louis Arena. He never left.

"Budd Lynch didn't just work for the Red Wings, he was part of the brand," former player and current Wings broadcaster Mickey Redmond told *USA Today* after Lynch died on October 9, 2012, at age 95.

"To me, he was a walking encyclopedia of not only life, but especially the hockey world. We're all better off for having the opportunity to work with him for so many years.

"He made a lot of people's lives better because of the way he was and the way he carried on. He had a great demeanor, a great, proud Irishman, and wore it on his sleeve. A real gentleman."

For millions of Wings fans, hearing Lynch on the PA was as much a part of winter as snow. His style was spare—he relayed information to his audience without becoming a cheerleader.

In 1985, Lynch was honored by the NHL Broadcasters Association with the Foster Hewitt Memorial Award at the Hockey Hall of Fame. Nine years later, Lynch was enshrined into the Michigan Sports Hall of Fame. In 2005, he was given the Ty Tyson Award for excellence in broadcasting by the Detroit Sports Broadcasters Association.

"Budd Lynch will forever be synonymous with the Detroit Red Wings," Red Wings GM Ken Holland said after Lynch's death. "He experienced it all in his 63 years with the organization, from the glory days of Howe, Lindsay, Abel, and Delvecchio all the way to the championship runs of Yzerman and Lidstrom. He had a vast knowledge of the game, and the stories he could tell would have anyone who loves the sport mesmerized for hours. Budd was one of a kind, not only in his talents as a broadcaster, but in the way he lived his life and the upbeat attitude he always carried. He will be sorely missed by everyone in the Red Wings family."